"Jen Smith has illuminated a blind spot present since the founding of Jungian psychology: the complex of finance, money, and economics. She also clears a path for using depth-psychological interpretation and wisdom to clarify the shadowy psychology of economics, with Greece, home of a rich and relevant mythology, as an example. This book is timely, emerging when economics has grown so powerful that it dominates global affairs like the giants and Titans of old."

Craig Chalquist, author of *Terrapsychological Inquiry and Myths Among Us.*

A Jungian and Mythological View of Economics

This book aims to re-vision economics by taking a Jungian view of the recent global economic crisis of the 2010s, focusing on Greece's challenging experience in particular.

Recognizing the genius loci of Greece by taking a terrapsychological approach allows Greece to be an active participant in the discussions rather than purely an object to be studied. Observing the crisis through the lenses of mythology, cultural complexes, and the God-image deepens the understanding of modern-day economics. These viewpoints reveal the unconscious and archetypal elements at play in the dysfunctions. Exposing the foundational issues is critical to redeeming economics and confirms the value in seeing socioeconomic issues from a Jungian perspective. The issues revealed through the exploration are not unique to Greece, but rather reflect many of the fundamental problems of the current global economic system. Thus, like its ancient myths, Greece's modern-day story of suffering has insights for today's world.

The audience for this book includes and extends beyond Jungian psychology, and will also appeal to some in the field of economics and those interested in the application of Jungian ideas to sociocultural issues.

Jennifer Degnan Smith (BA Economics, MA Applied Psychology) received her PhD in Jungian and Archetypal Studies from Pacifica Graduate Institute. Her focus is on the application of depth psychology to sociocultural issues, particularly those related to business, economics, and the natural world. Her many years of consulting in the U.S. and Europe supported the creation of healthy working environments and helping people to connect to their vocation. She also taught Organizational Behavior to undergraduate and graduate students. Jennifer spent considerable time in Greece studying ancient myth and modern culture.

Routledge Focus on Jung, Politics and Culture
Series Editor: Andrew Samuels

The Jung, Politics and Culture series showcases the 'political turn' in Jungian and Post-Jungian psychology. Established and emerging authors offer unique perspectives and new insights as they explore the connections between Jungian psychology and key topics - including national and international politics, gender, race and human rights.

Titles in the series:

Anti-Semitism and Analytical Psychology
Jung, Politics and Culture
Daniel Burston

A Depth Psychological Study of the Peace Symbol
Jung, Politics and Culture
Michelle Rivera-Clonch

Racial Legacies
Jung, Politics and Culture
Fanny Brewster & Helen Morgan

Torture Survivors in Analytic Therapy
Jung, Politics, Culture
Monica Luci

Climate Change, Environments of Uncertainty and Loss
Jung, Politics and Culture
Sarah D. Norton

A Jungian and Mythological View of Economics
Jung, Politics and Culture
Jennifer Degnan Smith

For a full list of titles in this series, please visit https://www.routledge.com/Focus-on-Jung-Politics-and-Culture/book-series/FJPC

A Jungian and Mythological View of Economics

Jung, Politics, and Culture

Jennifer Degnan Smith

Routledge
Taylor & Francis Group
LONDON AND NEW YORK

First published 2026
by Routledge
4 Park Square, Milton Park, Abingdon, Oxon OX14 4RN

and by Routledge
605 Third Avenue, New York, NY 10158

Routledge is an imprint of the Taylor & Francis Group, an informa business

British Library Cataloguing-in-Publication Data
A catalogue record for this book is available from the British Library

ISBN: 9781032805993 (hbk)
ISBN: 9781032806006 (pbk)
ISBN: 9781003497622 (ebk)

DOI: 10.4324/9781003497622

Typeset in Times New Roman
by codeMantra

For Greece and her people, ancient and modern, to whom we are all indebted.

For Dave, Danny, and Emma, who have taught me the importance of soul.

Contents

1 An Overview and an Author's View 1

2 A Depth Psychological View of Economics and Money 12

3 Experts' Views of the Global Financial Crisis 24

4 A Depth Psychological View of Place and Economics 35

5 A Wounded View 46

6 A Complex View 56

7 A God's View 69

8 A Transformative View 81

Index 93

1 An Overview and an Author's View

I realized the value of viewing economics through the lens of Carl G. Jung's psychological theory while spending time in Greece during the Global Financial Crisis (GFC). The deep recession of the 2010s was one of the most challenging times in recent history. Although the crisis was rooted in the U.S. housing market, few places on Earth remained unscathed; "its impact was seen worldwide from shuttered maquiladora factories in Mexico to the restructuring of regional savings and loan *cajas* in Spain and extended joblessness for migrant workers in China's Pearl River Delta" (International Monetary Fund, 2018, p. 84). Greece was particularly vulnerable and suffered tremendously.

I had no intention of examining the crisis; instead, I planned on spending my time in Greece, officially the Hellenic Republic, studying its ancient myths. However, it seemed Greece had other plans for me. When I set aside my tourist map and wandered the streets of Athens, it felt as if the city spoke to me about its dire situation. It drew my attention to information through synchronicities, stories, and images, including the abundant street art that partially eclipsed its ancient sites. I became fascinated by what was unfolding in the collective psyche because, as psychologist James Hillman (2006) argued, "Art is the response of the City to its own psychological condition; Art expresses how each city senses itself. In fact, art is its common sense" (p. 295).

Greece, especially Athens, seemed to show me crucial aspects of economic health and development, and not just its own. It pointed to fundamental problems in our global economic system and suggested ways to remedy them. Greece offered guidance on how economics should be transformed—how it could be re-visioned. Much of what Greece spoke about reflected Jung's ideas about psychological well-being, which should not be surprising. Jung held the ancient Greek people and their myths in high regard, recognizing the stories as sources of universal wisdom.

To be clear, I did **not** view Greece as a case study for applying Jungian psychology. Instead, it was quite the opposite. It felt as if Greece guided the conversation, offering insights on what must be done to tackle our modern economic challenges. Hillman (1996) noted, "particular places have singular

DOI: 10.4324/9781003497622-1

spirits, and they call us" (p. 124). Greece seemed to beckon to me. It provided guidance and wisdom, and I eventually trusted enough to follow.

The idea that the world is alive, ensouled, and capable of communicating with us contradicts the beliefs of much of the Western world. Our Cartesian culture teaches us that the world is inanimate and that humans are the sole possessors of wisdom. While Jung's psychology helps to dismantle the divides created by a Cartesian view, I felt uneasy about the process of listening to and following Greece's direction. I shared my doubts with a friend, who suggested I was being asked to follow Ariadne's red thread. In Greek mythology, Ariadne provided the hero Theseus with a ball of red yarn before he entered the labyrinth to slay the Minotaur. Theseus unrolled the yarn on his way to the center so he could find his way back out. When viewed metaphorically, the red thread represents the guiding soul in our lives. After my conversation with my friend, I took my dog, Zen, for a walk. After a few blocks, I noticed something ahead in the middle of the sidewalk. It was a spool of red thread. I needed no further convincing to heed the call of Greece.

This concise book explores the specific insights that Greece and the Global Financial Crisis offer to a Jungian re-visioning of economics. Some may question the value of reflecting on the crisis, considering it feels like a long time ago, and much has occurred since then, including a global pandemic. However, many scholars argue that the crisis also stimulated the problems we see in current politics; "the years after the crisis saw sharp increases in political polarization and the rise of populist movements on both the left and right in Europe and the U.S." (Mukunda, 2018, para. 2). Beaton (2019) contended that the grassroots fascist movement in Greece was "largely, if not entirely, a consequence of the 'crisis' and a response to the new conditions since 2010" (p. 385). Economics and politics are deeply intertwined.

Before delving into the specific insights from the Global Financial Crisis, it seems valuable to establish a foundation for the general relevance of Jung's psychology to socioeconomic health and development.

The Value of a Jungian View of Economics

Jung was, and still is, not without his critics. Jungian scholars have recognized how the culture of the early 20th century and Jung's own human flaws influenced his psychology and have been addressing the resulting issues. Despite his shortcomings, Jung was a visionary. He could see societal problems, including the harmful effects of technology, long before they became apparent.

Jung saw himself as a rational scientist, yet he had a keen interest in mythology, philosophy, comparative religion, literature, and the esoteric. He maintained that a "rational attitude to human psychology was not only inadequate but, in the light of history, preposterous" (Stevens, 1994, p. 1). Therefore, a Jungian approach to psychology recognizes the importance of the wisdom that arises from "non-rational" sources, such as mythology and the imagination. The information that emerges is also pertinent to economics since the economic system, for better or worse, is at least partially the product of the human psyche. Three aspects of Jung's psychology appear especially noteworthy in the context of economics.

Uncovers Unconscious Influences

The first is Jung's profound understanding of the nature of the psyche, especially the influence of the unconscious on people's lives. Jungian psychology is often referred to as depth psychology because it aims to explore what lies in the unknown depths of individuals and groups, including the reasons for cultural and institutional dysfunction. The field of economics, particularly Behavioral Economics, has started to recognize that people are not entirely rational in their behavior. Jung's psychology significantly contributes to understanding why individuals think, feel, and act as they do, particularly through his concept of complexes, which has entered the everyday vernacular.

People are criticized for such things as having a mother, hero, or victim complex; however, complexes are a normal part of human life. Everyone has complexes, including individuals and groups, often stemming from some form of wounding or trauma. Problems arise when complexes become activated. They create strong emotions and irrational behavior that resist logical thinking—something "comes over a person," causing them to lose control. As Jung (1948/1969d) argued, complexes have us; we do not have them. He believed their autonomy proved the limitations of the conscious mind and the existence of the unconscious: "Complexes are in truth the living units of the unconscious psyche, and it is only through them that we are able to deduce its existence and its constitution" (para. 210). Given the power of complexes on individuals and groups, it is critical to understand how they impact the creation and continuation of economic systems, as well as individual and group economic behavior, which will be explored throughout the book.

Complexes sit in the personal layer of the unconscious, which also holds repressed memories and unconscious beliefs, values, and biases that are deeply ingrained through our cultural and familial upbringing. This layer also contains aspects of ourselves we would prefer not to acknowledge, such as greed or jealousy. However, the unconscious also contains our "gold," meaning the strengths and talents we have disowned due to lack of acceptance from our family or culture.

Some of the gold in Western culture's patriarchal shadow is the powerful feminine, which has been shunned and dominated by the masculine. The feminine principles of compassion, collaboration, and care for the natural world have lost out to the masculine principles of competition and logic. In Jungian psychology, an essential part of psychological development involves engaging in shadow work, which entails making the unconscious conscious, acknowledging the problematic aspects of ourselves and our culture, and reconnecting with our gold.

Jung also acknowledged a second, deeper layer of the unconscious—the collective unconscious or objective psyche—which contains humanity's psychic heritage. This heritage "is not individual but common to all men, and perhaps even to all animals, and is the true basis of the individual psyche" (Jung, 1931/1969a, para. 321). Every person is born with this second layer, the realm of archetypes. Jung (1948/1969c) described archetypes as "modes of apprehension" (para. 280), meaning archetypes influence how we perceive and comprehend the world. They are the organs of the psyche. Individuals everywhere experience archetypes such as mother and father or the psychological experiences of death and rebirth, influenced by their cultural and personal histories. Archetypes fundamentally shape our world and lie at the core of our complexes. To grasp the strengths and dysfunctions of our economic system, we must uncover the archetypes at play in it.

The unconscious is often a source of problems. However, Jung also recognized it as a wellspring of inspiration, intuition, creativity, and imagination, which are critical to people's cultural and psychological lives. In ancient Greece, this paradox of the unconscious as a place of suffering and wealth was represented by Hades, the God and the realm of the Underworld. Hades evoked a sense of dread and fear. Nonetheless, Hades' symbol was the cornucopia because it was where the harvest was stored and represented a place of great abundance.

Jung (1948/1969c) recognized the presence and influence of the instinctual and biological elements of human life, including the more challenging aspects of humanity, such as greed and power, which clearly manifest in the economic system. Despite the efforts of most religious movements to suppress the less desirable aspects of the human condition, they cannot simply be repressed or prayed away. Instead, they must be confronted, and depth psychology offers guidance in doing so.

Therefore, Jung's work significantly contributes to understanding the workings of the psyche. This includes identifying the existence and nature of the unconscious and how it impacts people's individual and cultural lives. Jung's work provides insight into the depths of economic dysfunctions and presents a holistic path to development.

Promotes a Holistic and Systemic View of Economic Health and Development

Although developed for individual psychology, Jung's concept of individuation can be considered in the context of collective culture. Instead of perpetuating the notion that people should be perfect, individuation focuses on becoming whole; "I use the term 'individuation' to denote the process by which a person becomes a psychological 'in-dividual,' that is a separate, indivisible unity or 'whole'" (Jung, 1939/1969b, para. 490). The archetype of the Self is both the guiding force and the outcome of the process of individuation.

Individuation requires people to identify their uniqueness, undergo the often-painful process of unlearning many entrenched cultural beliefs, and decide for themselves what should be valued. As they move toward wholeness and their own distinctiveness, they balance and integrate different aspects of the psyche. This process is not done in isolation. It requires people to develop deeper relationships with themselves and those around them. Individuation is not sought purely for the individual's benefit; instead, it helps the entire society.

Examining economics through the lens of individuation is valuable because it challenges economics' foundations. It prompts economics to consider what it values, such as GDP growth and competition, along with what it neglects, such as environmental and mental health. Furthermore, it entails balance and diversity. Jung's psychology emphasizes the importance of recognizing what is repressed in both individuals and cultures. He asserted that a hyper-focus in one direction is problematic and can lead to a disruptive counterbalance.

Jung was concerned with Western culture's focus on rationalism and intellect, which prevents people from experiencing soulful and natural human lives (Sabini, 2002). He recognized Western culture's profound disregard for the feminine and the natural world. In cultural maturation and growth, Jungian psychology calls for redeeming these elements and returning them from the shadows. As culture is viewed as a whole, it also necessitates ensuring that all individuals experience economic well-being. No person or plant left behind.

Viewing economics through a Jungian lens requires individuals to recognize their role in economic issues. Collectively, this is often experienced in cultural complexes, which highlight a group's long-standing, unhealed wounds. These wounds can undermine a community's well-being, including its economic health. Addressing the damage communities have suffered, often for generations, is essential.

Jung argued that one gaping wound in Western culture—and a fundamental problem in our approach to economics—is our severance from an ensouled world.

Reconnects People to an Ensouled World

Perhaps one of Jung's greatest gifts to modern culture is reminding us of the sacredness of Nature, which Jung capitalized to reflect its divinity (Sabini, 2002). He believed Nature was composed of both spirit and matter. A tenet of depth psychology is the notion that people are deeply connected to an ensouled world, the anima mundi. The health of the planet cannot be separated from people's physical and psychological well-being.

Jung pointed out the harm that Christianity has inflicted on our relationship with Nature by perpetuating the belief that man is made in the image of God and, therefore, superior to the natural world. Christianity places the divine in the sky and no longer amongst the mountains and animals. Our economic system follows suit. Chalquist and Barnwell (2023) highlighted how the loss of the anima mundi has devastated the environment: "Colonialism, capitalism, extractivism—an economy based on the extraction of minerals and fossil fuels from the Earth—have pushed many ecosystems and the world itself to their limits" (p. 5).

Hillman (2006) argued that not only is the natural world ensouled, but so is everything created by human hands; "Not only animals and plants ensouled as in the Romantic vision, but soul is given with each thing, God-given things and man-made things of the street" (p. 33). Our current culture has a narcissistic relationship with Nature and objects. We value them based on what they provide for us. They are evaluated according to how much they feed our stomachs or our egos. Economics calls for a re-enchantment of our world rather than viewing it merely as a resource to be exploited.

Jung argued for the idea of the *unus mundus*, or one world, in which there is an underlying unity in which everything is connected. In many respects, Jung's ideas about the *unus mundus* reflect the new science paradigm, and he conversed extensively with the quantum physicist Wolfgang Pauli about an interconnected reality.

Jung (1954/1969f) argued that the *unus mundus* connects the material and spiritual realms experienced in the archetypes, which have both a psychic and a physical aspect:

> Since psyche and matter are contained in one and the same world, and moreover are in continuous contact with one another and ultimately rest on irrepresentable, transcendental factors, it is not only possible but fairly probable, even, that psyche and matter are two different aspects of one and the same thing.
>
> (para. 418)

Jung argued that archetypes are "the mediators of the *unus mundus*, responsible for organizing ideas and images in the psyche as well as for governing the fundamental principles of matter and energy in the physical world" (Stevens, 1994, p. 57). This reinforces the importance of considering the archetypal realm when discussing something as critical to our lives as our economic system. We can glimpse our inner worlds by paying attention to what is happening in the material world.

Thus, a Jungian approach to economics requires profound shifts in cultural attitudes and belief systems. It challenges the Cartesian idea of humans being separate from a mechanistic world and returns to the idea of an ensouled world. This change in perspective dramatically shifts the importance of the environment in economics. The need to care for the world would be felt through the heart rather than rationalized through the mind. A depth psychological approach would also consider the nuances of different places and communities as Jung acknowledged that places have essences or souls; "the old idea that every country or people has its own angel, just as the earth has a soul" (Jung, 1975, p. 432).

Jungian Sources of Information

A depth psychological view of economics also requires a shift in our understanding of information sources. To dive into the depths of the human psyche, we must stop colluding with the notion that all knowledge is procured through thinking and rationalization. The unconscious cannot be viewed directly; it speaks in a symbolic language. Attuning ourselves to the symbolic nature of the world demands imagination, which has lost out to the rational function in our culture. Yet, as Albert Einstein (2009), who occasionally met with Jung, stated, "Imagination is more important than knowledge. For knowledge is limited, whereas imagination embraces the entire world, stimulating progress, giving birth to evolution. It is, strictly speaking, a real factor in scientific research" (p. 97). Imagination is not merely fantasy but is a vital source of wisdom. The images emerging from the imaginal realm are rich with information, which will be discussed in the next chapter.

We must also learn the symbolic language of dreams and myths. Jung argued that dreams may be "commentaries on personal complexes" (Samuels, Shorter, & Plaut, 1986, p. 48). They illuminate the unconscious elements that run our lives. This applies to the dreams that visit people at night and the collective dreams that surface in cultural stories, whether ancient myths or Hollywood blockbusters. Ancient peoples engaged with myth to navigate their psychological lives. As Jung (1931/1969a) stated, "the whole of mythology could be taken as a sort of projection of the collective unconscious" (para. 325).

Hillman (1976) argued that the archetypes are the "*deepest patterns of psychic functioning*" and are "best comparable with a God" (p. xix). The ancient Greek pantheon of gods held the complexity of human experience. The archetypes come into view if we look at our lives and the situations we find ourselves in through a metaphorical and mythological lens; "Gods, religions sometimes say, are less accessible to the sense and to the intellect than they are to the imaginative vision and emotion of the soul" (pp. xix–xx). To understand economics, we must put on a metaphorical lens and seek out the gods and goddesses running it from the shadows.

We must also look at projections. Jung (1951/1969e) stated that people do not make projections, but rather, the unconscious puts its disowned aspects onto someone else, which changes "the world into the replica of one's own unknown face" (para. 17). Those things that aggravate us about other people and that we accuse them of are often aspects of ourselves that we cannot or do not want to see. This is true on a group level as well. What one group accuses the other of is often something they do not want to see in themselves. During the GFC, much blame was thrown around between countries and organizations, which frequently turned out to be shadow projections.

The unconscious is also experienced in synchronicities or meaningful coincidences, like mine with the red thread. Synchronicities involve the mirroring of internal and external events that are not causally related and are usually accompanied by strong emotional reactions. They bring physical form and experience to the psyche's unconscious concerns and insights. Synchronicities most profoundly demonstrate the existence of the *unus mundus*.

Jung argued that synchronicities serve as a compensatory function that rebalances a one-sidedness. They act as a "dialogue between the self and the world, between our rational mind and the mind of nature" (Le Grice, 2010, p. 127). They provide us with guidance and meaning:

> It is as if the extraordinary coincidence of certain events, or the uncanny correlation between something external that happens to us with our own internal states of consciousness, is actually attempting to convey a meaningful message of great personal significance.
>
> (p. 126)

Thus, depth psychology offers a form of night vision—providing a view into the darkness of the unconscious, which allows for its transformation.

A Jungian Approach to the Global Financial Crisis

Greece's angel—its unique soul—pointed to three critical areas in the revisioning of economics, which form the basis of this book.

Chapter 4 builds on Jung's ideas about the anima mundi and the *unus mundus*. In economics, places are generally evaluated by their natural resources and geographical locations. Depth psychology significantly broadens the view of place, including historical and cultural elements and its unique essence. This is critical to the economic health of individual places and their residents.

Chapters 5 and 6 build on Jung's idea about trauma and complexes and explore their presence in the GFC. Problematic aspects of the U.S. and Greek economies point to unhealed collective trauma, which suggests a need to incorporate cultural healing into economic health and development.

Open wounds are often the foundation of complexes. Thomas Singer and Samuel Kimbles (2004) extended Jung's theory of complexes to understand group behavior. Cultural complexes create an inner sociology for the group and are passed down for generations. They can be destructive to the collective and thus are essential to explore because they help to understand conflicts and issues within a culture. Considering a group's cultural complexes helps to understand their economic behavior and reveals the dysfunctions of the current economic system. Depth psychology also provides ways to lessen the impact of complexes.

Chapter 7 explores the impact of the God-image on economics. Depth psychology is not focused on the metaphysical aspects of a higher power but instead on the idea that "'God' is a psychological fact" (Corbett, 1996, p. 39). The God-image reflects what is of the utmost importance in the human psyche. It also impacts what people value and worship, consciously and unconsciously, and their beliefs about their role and purpose in this life. It also influences their thoughts about the sources of power and the amount of control they have. A culture's God-image significantly impacts the values and functioning of its economic system.

Before exploring these three areas in detail, two chapters will continue laying down some foundations. Chapter 2 will review some key ideas that depth psychologists have about economics and money, including how psychologically volatile money is. This chapter also reflects how depth psychologists' concerns about our current economic system align with some of the countercultural movements within the field of economics itself.

Chapter 3 presents an overview of the Global Financial Crisis of the 2010s, including a deep dive into Greece's experience. Economics is often criticized for being too theoretical and far removed from the realities of people's lives. Thus, looking at the GFC will bring economics back down to Earth. There is also value in looking back. Western culture's incessant drive to race forward into the future often prevents it from gaining insight from reflection and moving ahead with the wisdom of experience. There is much to be learned from the crisis. Reviewing the GFC exposes many problematic aspects of the global economic system and reflects how deeply intertwined the global economy is.

The Author's Lens

My interest in economics began at university. My original career plan was to pursue a career in economics to help countries advance in ways that were not solely focused on GDPs and feeding the coffers, but instead on feeding the soul and environmental and sociological health. I also had a desire to appreciate a place's uniqueness and to stay loyal to its people, which makes me a fellow pagan with Hillman (1996), who defined pagans as a "people of place, as defenders of place against the alienation brought by monotheism" (p. 123). In this case, it was the monotheism of growing GDPs. My plan was disrupted, but I finally returned to that endeavor years later while studying Jung's psychology.

Despite Western culture's aspiration for objectivity, it is impossible to achieve. I appreciate that my perspective shapes and colors this book. I am not Greek, although once, while discussing parenting styles with my Greek friends, they told me I would make a great Greek mother. Not being Greek holds me at a disadvantage in some ways, yet it also provides a different view. Rasche (2016) noted that it is also difficult to see a cultural complex clearly within a culture because the intense emotions accompanying a complex can influence one's perspective. Thus, I add some outside perspectives. However, it is often difficult to understand a cultural complex from outside a culture because it can seem foreign. Thus, in exploring the GCF and Greece's crisis, I did not rely on my opinion but extensively researched expert views. I read and listened to people from various fields, some of whom were Greek and others who were not, but all of whom deeply understood the people and their experiences. I also endeavored to circle the crisis from various perspectives to understand the whole story. I started with my view of the crisis while considering what other scholars had to say about the relationship between psychology and economics.

References

Beaton, R. (2019). *Greece: Biography of a modern nation*. Allen Lane.

Chalquist, C., & Barnwell, G. (2023). Introduction: Everything converses. In C. Chalquist & G. Barnwell (Eds.), *Terrapsychology: Further inquiry into self, place, and planet* (pp. 1–10). Routledge.

Corbett, L. (1996). *The religious function of the psyche*. Routledge.

Einstein, A. (2009). *Einstein on cosmic religion and other opinions and aphorisms*. Dover Publications.

Hillman, J. (1976). *Re-visioning psychology*. Harper & Row.

Hillman, J. (1996). Psychology-monotheistic or polytheistic: Twenty-five years later. *Spring*, *60*, 111–125.

Hillman, J. (2006). *City & soul*. R. J. Leaver (Ed.). Spring Publications, Inc.

International Monetary Fund Research Department. (2018, October 09). Chapter 2: The global economic recovery 10 years after the 2008 financial meltdown. In International Monetary Fund staff, *World Economic Outlook: Challenges to steady growth* (pp. 71–100). International Monetary Fund, Publication Services. https://www.imf.org/en/Publications/WEO/Issues/2018/09/24/world-economic-outlook-october-2018

Jung, C. G. (1969a). The structure of the psyche (R. F. C. Hull, Trans.). In H. Read et al. (Eds.), *The collected works of C. G. Jung* (Vol. 8, 2nd ed., pp. 139–158). Princeton University Press (Original work published 1931).

Jung, C. G. (1969b). Conscious, unconscious, and individuation (R. F. C. Hull, Trans.). In H. Read et al. (Eds.), *The collected works of C.G. Jung* (Vol. 9 pt. 1, 2nd ed., pp. 275–289). Princeton University Press (Original work published 1939).

Jung, C. G. (1969c). Instinct and the unconscious (R. F. C. Hull, Trans.). In H. Read et al. (Eds.), *The collected works of C. G. Jung* (Vol. 8, 2nd ed., pp. 129–138). Princeton University Press (Original work published 1948).

Jung, C. G. (1969d). A review of the complex theory (R. F. C. Hull, Trans.). In H. Read et al. (Eds.), *The collected works of C.G. Jung* (Vol. 8, 2nd ed., pp. 92–104). Princeton University Press (Original work published 1948).

Jung, C. G. (1969e). Aion: Researches into the phenomenology of the self (R. F. C. Hull, Trans.). In H. Read et al. (Eds.), *The collected works of C.G. Jung* (Vol. 9 pt. 2, 2nd Ed.). Princeton University Press (Original work published 1951).

Jung, C. G. (1969f). On the nature of the psyche (R. F. C. Hull, Trans.). In H. Read et al. (Eds.), *The collected works of C.G. Jung* (Vol. 8, 2nd ed., pp. 159–234). Princeton University Press (Original work published 1954).

Jung, C. G. (1975). Letters: 1951–1961 (R. F. C. Hull, Trans.) In G. Adler (Ed.), *C. G. Jung letters II*. Princeton University Press.

Le Grice, K. (2010). *The archetypal cosmos: Rediscovering the gods in myth, science and astrology*. Floris Books.

Mukunda, G. (2018, September 25). The social and political costs of the financial crisis, 10 years later. *Harvard Business Review*. https://hbr.org/2018/09/the-social-and-political-costs-of-the-financial-crisis-10-years-later

Rasche, J. (2016). Introduction. In J. Rasche & T. Singer (Eds.), *Europe's many souls: Exploring cultural complexes and identities* (pp. 15–31). Spring Journal, Inc.

Sabini, M. (Ed.). (2002). *The earth has a soul: C.G. Jung on nature, technology & modern life*. North Atlantic Books.

Samuels, A., Shorter, B., & Plaut, F. (1986). *A critical dictionary of Jungian analysis*. Routledge.

Singer, T., & Kimbles, S. L. (Eds.). (2004). *The cultural complex: Contemporary Jungian perspectives on psyche and society*. Routledge.

Stevens, A. (1994). *Jung: A very short introduction*. Oxford University Press.

2 A Depth Psychological View of Economics and Money

A View from Hell

Depth psychologists recognize the potential in the Western world's economic system, which combines capitalism and socialism. However, they also argue that human fallibilities have derailed that potential. Hillman (2006) was particularly scathing: "Of all the fallen fields of human endeavor, economics must take first place, which therefore locates its high priests on Hell's lowest ring" (p. 362). This places economic leaders on the ninth circle of Dante's Inferno, alongside those being punished for treachery, betraying humanity, and acts of hubris against the divine. The high priests find themselves next to Satan, Cain, Judas Iscariot, and Brutus and Cassius frozen in a lake—the appropriate punishment for their cold-hearted crimes.

Hillman joins a chorus of voices from various disciplines, including economics, arguing that our obsession with growth and competition leaves much of humanity and the natural world neglected. Growing GDPs do not assuage mental health issues, homelessness, addiction, and ecological disasters. While business growth and profits continue to soar, so does work stress, job dissatisfaction, and income disparity. Bigger is not always proving to be better.

Samuels (2014) expressed strong concerns about the modern economic system:

> Because of economic thinking and economic practices, people are suffering and dying every day. Anyone with a conscience has to try to evaluate what is going on in the economic sphere. Economics is the filter or culvert through which the vicissitudes of power, in all their complexity and cruelty, are passed. Where economics goes, violent conflict often follows. (p. 79)

Donning a mythological lens, Kipnis (2013) argued that we are caught in a Midas complex where "no amount of material acquisition brings personal fulfillment and where our pursuit of wealth paradoxically increases our suffering instead of bringing us the liberation we ultimately seek" (p. 2). The obsession

DOI: 10.4324/9781003497622-2

with money comes at the expense of everything else, including clean water and fertile land, reflecting how King Midas became famished when he turned everything he touched into gold.

Economics fills the religious void, guiding people's daily lives and providing a sense of purpose. Hillman (2012) compared economics to a monotheistic god with omnipotence but lacking compassion or soul: "I think we're miserable partly because we have only one god, and that's economics. Economics is a slave-driver" ("Conversations," para. 109). Economics sold its soul to science and its singular focus on growth (Hillman, 2006). Economics' pursuit of cost efficiency leaves room for little else: "Cheapness becomes the bottom line, and the huge cost is aesthetic, ecological, psychological, spiritual—the very quality of life, the soul of life" (p. 301).

Stoknes (2009) argued that the current financial system depends on someone willing to take on new debt, widening the gap between the rich and poor. Debt brings in constraint; "the Norwegian word for debt is *gjeld*, and comes from the Old Norse *gelda*, which also means to geld or castrate" and causes the debtor to be "neutered as an economic player" (p. 168). This process continues the transfer of wealth from poor to rich countries as the "international monetary system's interest claims become a form of structural violence exercised against these populations" (p. 171). It becomes a form of neo-colonialism.

Credit fuels the imagination. People want money to live the lives they imagine (Hillman, 2006; Stoknes, 2009). Hillman even argued that we should "*define money as that which 'possibilizes' the imagination*" (p. 359). However, credit can also give energy to people's instincts, allowing them to buy impulsively to gratify ego desires. Debt, in its constraint, may also force people to consider the reality of their situation and take responsibility. They may be required to engage the imagination to innovate as frequently "necessity is the mother of invention."

Thus, it seems that economics and the psyche have deep ties:

> Economics has so taken over the language of psychology that we have to look at economic news to read our national mental state. Inflated or depressed? Sluggish or expansive? What way is 'interest' going? We watch the charts and hear the prognostics to discover what the collective soul is feeling.
>
> (Hillman, 2006, p. 300)

Despite these problems, economics and money do not have to be detrimental. They have ties to sacred aspects of life. Flowers (2000) argued that economics' global interconnections reflect a systemic worldview. Economics provides the opportunity for evolution and can be a "*continual re-creation of possibility*" (p. 211).

Depth psychologists identified ways to tap into these possibilities. Before diving further into their insights, two Jungian concepts—soul and image—require exploration. Soul and image rarely appear in the context of an approach to economics that is focused on data and growth. However, there is plenty of space for them in discussions about psychological and environmental health. Moreover, describing Jung's psychology without speaking about soul and image is almost impossible.

Soul and Image

Jung honored the Greek meaning of the word psyche, which is soul, rather than equating the psyche with the mind. Theologians and philosophers have struggled to define the soul for millennia, perhaps reflecting soul's elusive nature. From a Jungian perspective, soul is present in the individual and the collective, yet it extends beyond the human, having divine connections and immortality:

> The individual soul, with its conflicts, heights, depths, and uniqueness; the collective soul, the world soul, one's sense of humanness shared with others; and the transpersonal, supra-individual soul of the metaphysicians and theologians, soul in the spiritual and religious sense, as a manifestation of the mind of God, the objective psyche beyond human understanding.
>
> (Hopcke, 1989, p. 38)

Thus, Jung saw soul as something more extensive than the individual. The psyche is not within people, but rather, people are in psyche or soul. Jung also argued that the soul is in an "intermediate position" belonging to the human and the spirit worlds. Thus, "the soul always has an earthly as well as a rather ghostly quality" (Jung, 1971, para. 425). Caring for the soul is critical to a meaningful life. Jung argued that our culture lost its soul when it moved from a life focused on the mythical and symbolic to the materialistic. This is undoubtedly true of economics.

Hillman (1976) continued to develop Jung's idea of soul and called for the experience of soul-making, which makes soul a "perspective rather than a substance" (p. xvi). We make meaning of our lives by viewing them through an imaginal and metaphorical lens;

> The human adventure is a wandering through the vale of the world for the sake of making soul. Our life is psychological, and the purpose of life is to make psyche of it, to find connections between life and soul.
>
> (p. xv)

Soul is in the metaxy, in the in-between. Soul exists "between us and events, between the doer and the deed" (Hillman, 1976, p. xvi). More than anything, soul reveals itself in images and through the imagination.

Soul speaks through images. The unconscious, including the archetypes, can be accessed through images. Through images, "the soul conveys the forces of the unconscious to consciousness; it is both receiver and transmitter, an organ for perceiving unconscious contents" (Jung, 1971, para. 425). In depth psychological terms, images are visual, auditory, emotional, or sensory. They may appear in all aspects of our lives, whether in art, our dreams, or our day-to-day living. Unfortunately, contemporary Western culture has dismissed the power of images; when they are considered from a solely rational perspective, images are perceived as worthless (para. 426).

Hillman (2005) went even further, arguing that "the hatred of the image, the fear of its power, and of the imagination is very old and very deep in our culture" (p. 73). He blamed the Council in Constantinople in 869 and the one in Nicaea in 787 for changing the concept of human nature from being composed of spirit, soul, and body to one of just being spirit (mind) and body. Soul—the world of images that resides in the valleys and the vales—lost out to spirit, which takes people to intellectual heights and out of the human experience and the imagination.

To experience the wisdom of the image, we must consider its details with a metaphorical eye. Images are "faces to be read as displays of soul" (Hillman, 2006, p. 143). Through images, we experience the world's soul. By slowing down and noticing the details, "our personal psyches are in tune with the presentation of the world's soul" (p. 144).

Money is in the place of soul because money is somewhere between the spiritual and material (Hillman, 2006, p. 360). Money holds the soul in the vales, in the concreteness of life. Because money and soul are so profoundly tied, we need to look at the money complex to understand the souls of modern people (Hillman, 2006). We can comprehend the money complex by looking at the images around economics and money.

Money's Changing Cultural Images

Our culture influences how we see money, and money reflects culture (Stoknes, 2009; Hillman, 2006). Samuels (2014) noted that our economic systems reflect our culture's ideas about human nature and are heavily influenced by past experiences (p. 81). Money provides a means for communal life by "giving things of the world a value held in common by the community" (Schenk, 2012, p. 153). If we change what we value, we can change the economic system and vice versa.

The images around money and economics reflect cultural values. Originally, money was tied to the divine and Nature. Money was named after Moneta, the Latin goddess of memory, which also means to warn or admonish (Schenk, 2012, p. 152). Greek coins with images of animals, Nature, and gods and goddesses were some of the first forms of money (Hillman, 2006; Kipnis, 2013; Schenk, 2012; Stoknes, 2009). However, over time, the images on money changed to monarchs and emperors, which moved money to the realm of humans and power, taking it further away from the more soulful elements (Hillman, 2006; Stoknes, 2009). Hillman blamed many of today's economic problems on money's disconnect from Nature and the gods, where its archetypal foundation sits; "the ugliness, the power corruption, the purely quantitative nature of money today is not money's fault, but that of its having been severed and then fallen from the Gods from which it came" (Hillman, p. 362).

Over the last few years, money has continued to move further from the Earth and the gods, becoming even less visible and tangible as most exchanges are done electronically (Kipnis, 2013). Cash, the physical, soulful incarnation of money, is often perceived as "dirty" and associated with the underground economy (Kipnis). Money is taken from our hands and placed in the spiritual heights of the cloud and cryptocurrencies. We only know how much of it we have from the numbers on the screens of our devices.

The scholars also highlight how Christianity has done a number on our relationship with money by putting money and soul in opposition (Hillman, 2006; Stoknes, 2009). Money is portrayed as sinful or evil, as seen in the bible verse from Luke 8:25: "For it is easier for a camel to enter in through a needle's eye than for a rich man to enter into the kingdom of heaven" (Hillman, p. 356). Stoknes (2009) noted the importance that was placed on Jesus being poor in Luke: "It is the poor person who has the ability to donate out of a rich soul. The rich person is hardened by money and ends up with an impoverished soul" (p. 37). However, this religious teaching is not lived within many religious institutions. The Roman Catholic Church is considered one of the world's wealthiest institutions, with the Church of Scientology and the Latter-day Saint church not far behind.

Interestingly, during the Global Financial Crisis, the Greek people revisited the connection between the divine and money. In 2011, the National Archaeological Museum in Athens, along with the Numismatic Museum and Alpha Bank, one of the largest banks in Greece, put together an exhibit highlighting the connections between coinage and myth and the importance of the imaginal. The group also put on another exhibit at the Cycladic Museum, *Money: Tangible Symbols in Ancient Greece*, in 2017. Both exhibits reflected much of what Hillman (2006) and Stoknes (2009) noted about the early connections of money to Nature and gods and later connections to humans and power. Kaltsas (2011), the director of the National Archaeological Museum in Athens, noted the

> elevation of the Hellenistic kings to the rank of hero and of their deeds and feats to the realm of myth, as taught by the practice of Alexander the Great, legitimized their installation in the obverse type of the coins, which until then was an exclusively privileged space for the representation of gods and heroes.
>
> (p. 21)

The exhibits recognized that money was not merely functional but a means of artistic expression. In antiquity, coins were related to iconography and symbolic carriers for religious, political, and economic messages. Images were also put on coins to appease the Nature gods and to depict the deities and myths of the local area. Coins were also crucial to the ancient cities as coins "also formed a basic testimony for a city, its governance, the issuing authority, economic transactions, trade, artistic trends, and technical achievements" (Evgenidou, 2011, p. 13). Many of the rulers in ancient Greece used specific images of the gods on coins to promote "their authority through the adoption of specific divine or heroic traits and attributes [which] distinguished them not only from common people but also among their peers" (Tselekas, 2011, p. 244).

The exhibits served as a reminder of Greece's role in creating and distributing some of the world's first coins. Given the focus on the coins' original connections to the gods, Nature, and the imaginal, perhaps, during a time of great despair, the Greek people needed to be reminded that money could serve the soul and the divine. Perhaps the people were also considering the forces shaping modern money. This deliberation was seen in a street art image in Athens by the artist Oré featuring a melting Greek Euro coin with the question, "From ancient to modern times, who controls the money?"

Is power held by the government, organizations, religions, people, or the gods? Depth psychologists glimpsed some of the archetypal elements at play in today's economic system.

The Gods of Modern-Day Economics

It takes little experience wearing a mythological lens to see the gods and the archetypal influences in our economic system. Saturn, sometimes known as Kronos, sits high on his throne as King of the Titans. He devoured his children because he feared losing his power to them. Saturn has strong associations with money; "Saturn governs coins, minting, and wealth" (Hillman, 2005, p. 44). He is also known for being greedy, miserly, and tyrannical, not to mention gluttonous, and a reflection of Ebenezer Scrooge in Charles Dickens's *A Christmas Carol* (Stoknes, 2009, p. 127). Saturn is about the intellect and reason and has little connection to the emotional or the feminine (Hillman, 2005), which is often one of the criticisms of economics.

Psychologically, the Titanic reflects "the gigantism of the psyche—inflation, grandiosity, unchecked haste" that usually moves from a power trip to a great fall (Slater, 1998, p. 107). The King of the Titans, brimming with hubris and disregarding the divine, leads economics and business in the charge for bigger and better and more market share and GDP growth.

Apollo, the handsome god of light and clarity and the favored son of Zeus, is also seen in economics. Apollo is the god of industriousness and civilization as he "wakes us each from our sleep and cheers us on to our work" (Hillman,

2007, p. 324). Stoknes (2009) argued that economic theory encompasses Apollo, whose "cool intellect allows man to raise himself above the world, observe things at a distance, try to acquire perspective via logical methods and seek to shed light on contexts and 'mountains of data'" (p. 193). Apollo keeps economics in the spiritual heights and the rational world and far away from the soul and the emotional. Apollo brings with him some necessary skills, but his shadow side is unreasonable, arrogant, and judgmental (Stoknes, 2009). His dominance also leaves his counterpart, Hermes, the god of the marketplace, business, boundaries, communication, and thievery, in the shadows.

Hermes' negative aspects, such as his tricksterish and dishonest behavior, which are rife in business and economics, will be discussed in the upcoming chapters. However, his more positive attributes are repressed by the dominance of Apollo. Hermes is the archetypal pattern of "transactions going on in all markets every day" (Stoknes, 2009, p. 101). He is not solely concerned with making a deal but is also invested in innovation and his social relationships. Stoknes argued that "the dismal science" of economics, so named by Thomas Carlyle, is more focused on serious numbers and analysis, missing Hermes's energy, humor, and playfulness (pp. 106–107).

Stoknes (2009) recognized the presence of the Goddess Ananke in the growth of debt in the global economic system, which has become a yoke around the neck of many countries. Ananke was the goddess of bonds, rules, and restraint. She was called necessity, and the "Greeks shuddered to think of the name" (p. 176).

Saturn, Apollo, and Ananke leave little room for other gods and goddesses, particularly those with ties to the emotional, the feminine, beauty, and the natural world. Their absence will be discussed in the following chapters. However, it is worth pointing out here that Hestia, the goddess of the hearth and home, is sorely missing. Hestia's presence entails a concern for the health of the economy of the family and the need to live within one's means, and ecological problems are part of the consequence of ignoring Hestia as the world around us deteriorates (Paris, 1986).

Interestingly, the etymology of the word economics comes from ancient Greek, *oikonomia*: *oikos* (household) and (*nemein*), akin to management and dispensation (Lesham, 2016). Thus, initially, economics was about the home and not solely about the workplace. Lesham noted there are significant differences between ancient *oikonomia* and modern economics. The ancient Greeks believed:

> The main task of economic rationality is to advance the good life as they understood it, which means support for philosophy, for involvement in public life, and also for not giving in to what they viewed as the unnatural urge to pursue economic goals or luxuries for their own sake.
>
> (p. 226)

The ancient Greek approach to economics was different from the one today. Depth psychologists have identified ways to fix some of the problems of modern-day economics and return it to its original intentions, perhaps to its archetypal roots.

Curing the Problems of Economics

As noted in the last chapter, Jung's psychology offers many insights into curing problems in the economic system, including the need to own our part of the shadow. Samuels (2014) argued that it is easy to blame an unjust system, but we must recognize our role in contributing to the ongoing stench of economics. We must all do our own bit of shadow work (p. 83).

We must also be prepared to sacrifice aspects of the ego to enable psychological growth and make room for the soul (Samuels, 2014). Flowers (2000) acknowledged that our current economic myth perpetuates self-interest as a primary motivation, prohibiting self-sacrifice. Kipnis (2013) also called for dethroning the ego when he argues for radical altruism as an antidote to the Midas complex: "Radical altruists do not seem to hold the fantasy that their wealth somehow makes them superior to others" (p. 244). Rather than feeding the ego, wealth should be used to help humanity and Nature. There should be a focus on cooperation instead of competition.

Samuels (2014) also touched on the need for cooperation when he suggests denationalizing the psyche, "getting out of the Western box" by stopping the pattern in which we are "educated to think like states" (p. 87). By reimagining ourselves as nomads and becoming more empathic toward other people and groups, we can shift our worldview by sacrificing some of our identity and sense of security.

Stoknes (2009) built on Jung's idea of the problematic nature of one-sidedness. Economics is heavily skewed toward the masculine and logical. Stoknes called a move from the monotheism of an Apollonian approach to economics to a polytheistic approach, poly-capitalism, which adds other gods and goddesses to the pantheon. This would move economics from focusing on rationality, utility, and growth to valuing the environment, social cohesion, and soul. Money gives us something to live on, but the soul gives us something to live for (p. 252). Money and soul do not have to be opposites but can be found in each other; we must consider how "money can serve the soul" (p. 43).

Stoknes (2009) noted that our current economy could adopt an approach like Rhea, the daughter of the mother goddess Gaia. This approach allows flow and the natural cycles of life instead of linear growth and hoarding (p. 128). Thus, by considering what gods and goddesses are missing from economics, we can find options for re-visioning our economic system.

Jungian Connections to Other Economic Movements

Jungian thought aligns with other movements seeking to reform economic theory and practice, including some within economics itself. For instance, for several decades, feminist economics has sought to expose how economic models and approaches are masculine-oriented and contain "biases which give market relations pride of place over family and social relations, emphasize heroic individualism while ignoring interdependence, and define rationality so narrowly that even verbal analysis is excluded leave the discipline impoverished" (Ferber & Nelson, 2003, p. vii). Feminist economics argues for the need to expand economics to include more of the feminine principle, including the role of family, connections, and emotions. The need to account for "the contributions of all producers—including rural women" in GDP has been argued since the beginning of GDP calculations (Messac, 2018). Hestia needs to be restored to her rightful place.

Ecological economics is also working to undo the problems of modern-day economics by acknowledging that our biosphere is finite and the focus on economic growth is not sustainable. Ecological economics also appreciates the deep connection between humans and the natural world. It fosters "transformation towards an equitable and ecologically sustainable society with respect for the rights of people and nature, biological and cultural diversity" (International Society for Ecological Economics, n.d., para. 1). Ecological economics would appreciate the need for Rhea and other gods and goddesses with ties to the natural world.

Rethinking Economics, a global student network, is challenging the monopoly of neoclassical economics and its focus on growth, arguing that a "more pluralist approach can help economics to become both more effective and more democratic" and address social and ecological issues (Rethinking Economics & The New Weather Institute, 2017, p. 1). The group maintains that economics' connection to and impact on the natural world needs to be reflected in theory and practice. Like depth psychologists, they argue that politics, government, and culture influence economics. They also point out that markets are more complex than neoclassical economics recognizes. Finance and banking are highly influential, and economics needs to understand credit, debt, and failures in the system. The distribution of wealth, including the tendency toward increasing inequality, must be incorporated into economics. The group also argued that universal economic principles may not work across all nations. These countercultural movements within economics are well aligned with the psychology of Jung, who was quite accustomed to swimming against the prevailing tides of thought.

Rethinking Economics and the field of behavioral economics also recognize the need to better understand human behavior. Over recent decades, behavioral economics has become popular by integrating insights from psychology and challenging the neoclassical idea that people are rational in their economic decision-making. Behavioral economics has integrated some aspects of traditional social psychology. It considers rational and "irrational" aspects of decision-making, such as emotions, the social environment, instincts, memories, and unconscious biases. Depth psychology also recognizes the influence of these unconscious elements, particularly in the presence of complexes.

One way in which behavioral economics and depth psychology differ is in their understanding of intuition. Kahneman (2011) argued that there are two selves, or cognitive systems, that influence how we think. The first is quick, automatic, intuitive, and emotional, influenced by unconscious biases and memories. The second is much slower, analytical, more logical, and deliberate, and within our control. Kahneman believed that it is the role of the second to avoid the inherent issues in the first system as it is often flawed. He relied on Herbert Simon's definition from his research on chess masters, stating that "the situation has provided a cue; this cue has given the expert access to information stored in memory, and the information provides the answer. Intuition is nothing more and nothing less than recognition" (Simon, 1992, p. 155).

For depth psychologists, intuition is not simply dependent on patterns of experience; rather, it can be a creative process filled with wisdom if used with discernment. As Jung (1960/1971) said, "intuition is a kind of instinctive apprehension" and "its contents have the character of being 'given,' in contrast to the 'derived' or 'produced'" (para. 770). Unlike Kahneman, who splits thinking into intuition and analytical, depth psychology appreciates the value of both styles.

The economist Brendan Markey-Towler (2017) recognized the value of Jung's work, arguing that the economy should do more than meet basic desires; it should also be considered something that adds meaning to our lives, moving us toward self-actualization. He noted that Jung's concepts of archetypes and complexes influence economic behavior, and looking at people's personal mythologies can help explain their economic behavior.

Markey-Towler (2018) drew on Jung and Campbell's work with the hero archetype to describe the core archetype of human civilization as the "antifragile" personality, which "seeks and incorporates new knowledge they did not previously have so that their knowledge grows in the presence of radical uncertainty" (p. 6), which is an essential part of adapting to a changing socio-economic system (p. 8).

Therefore, it is becoming evident how Jung's psychology can offer insights into challenges within our current economic system and guidance on reimagining it. Depth psychologists and the countermovements in economics seem to address some of the same concerns and align with many of their recommendations for change, which will be examined more closely in the context of the Global Financial Crisis.

References

Conversations with a remarkable man: Honoring the late James Hillman. (2012, July). *The Sun*. Retrieved from https://www.thesunmagazine.org/issues/439/conversations-with-a-remarkable-man

Evgenidou, D. (2011). Acknowledgements. In D. Tsangari (Ed.), *Myth and coinage: Representations, symbolisms and interpretations from the Greek mythology* (pp. 11–15). Alpha Bank, National Archaeological Museum, Numismatic Museum.

Ferber, M., & Nelson, J. (2003). *Feminist economics today: Beyond economic man*. The University of Chicago Press.

Flowers, B. S. (2000). Practicing politics in the economic myth. In T. Singer (Ed.), *The vision thing: Myth, politics and psyche in the world* (pp. 207–212). Routledge.

Hillman, J. (1976). *Re-visioning psychology*. Harper & Row.

Hillman, J. (2005). *Senex & puer*. G. Slater (Ed.). Spring Publications.

Hillman, J. (2006). *City & soul*. R. J. Leaver (Ed.). Spring Publications.

Hillman, J. (2007). *Mythic figures*. Spring Publications, Inc.

Hopcke, R. H. (1989). *A guided tour of the collected works of C.G. Jung*. Shambhala.

International Society for Ecological Economics. (n.d.). Welcome to the international society for ecological economics. Retrieved from https://www.isecoeco.org/

Jung, C. G. (1971). The collected works of C. G. Jung: Vol. 6. Psychological types (R. F. C. Hull, Trans.). H. Read et al. (Eds.). Princeton University Press (Original work published 1921).

Kahneman, D. (2011). *Thinking, fast and slow*. Farrar, Straus and Giroux.

Kaltsas, N. (2011). Introduction. In D. Tsangari (Ed.), *Myth and coinage: Representations, symbolisms and interpretations from the Greek mythology* (pp. 20–26). Alpha Bank, National Archaeological Museum, Numismatic Museum.

Kipnis, A. R. (2013). *The Midas complex: How money drives us crazy and what we can do about it*. Indigo Phoenix Books.

Lesham, D. (2016). Retrospectives: What did the ancient Greeks mean by Oikonomia? *Journal of Economic Perspectives*, *30*(1), 225–231. https://pubs.aeaweb.org/doi/pdfplus/10.1257/jep.30.1.225

Markey-Towler, B. (2017). The economy as self-actualisation: Jungian economic psychology. Retrieved from https://medium.com/@brendanmarkeytowler/the-economy-as-self-actualisation-jungian-economic-psychology-669f0bd451fb

Markey-Towler, B. (2018). Antifragility, the black swan and psychology. *Evolutionary and Institutional Economics Review*, *15*, 367–384. Retrieved from https://link.springer.com/article/10.1007/s40844-018-0097-6

Messac, L. (2018, June 22). History tells us we've got GDP wrong. Here's why. World Economic Forum. Retrieved from https://www.weforum.org/stories/2018/06/women-s-unpaid-work-must-be-included-in-gdp-calculations-lessons-from-history/

Paris, G. (1986). *Pagan meditations: Aphrodite, Hestia, Artemis*. Spring Publications.

Rethinking Economics & the New Weather Institute. (2017, December 12). Theses for economic reformation. Retrieved from https://www.rethinkeconomics.org/wp-content/uploads/2023/10/33-Theses-for-an-Economics-Reformation.pdf

Samuels, A. (2014). Economics, psychotherapy and politics. *International Review of Sociology*, *24*(1), 77–90.

Schenk, R. (2012). *American soul: A cultural narrative*. Spring Journal Books.

Simon, H. (1992). What is an "explanation" of behavior? *Psychological Science, 3*(3). https://journals.sagepub.com/doi/abs/10.1111/j.1467-9280.1992.tb00017.x

Slater, G. (1998). Re-sink the Titanic. *Spring, 62*, 104–120.

Stoknes, P. E. (2009). *Money & soul: The psychology of money and the transformation of capitalism* (S. M. Davies, Trans.). Green Books (Original work published 2009).

Tselekas, P. (2011). Identification of rulers with gods and heroes. In D. Tsangari (Ed.), *Myth and coinage: Representations, symbolisms and interpretations from the Greek mythology* (pp. 244–247). Alpha Bank, National Archaeological Museum, Numismatic Museum.

3 Experts' Views of the Global Financial Crisis

Condensing the Global Financial Crisis into a single chapter is a Herculean task. Experts and scholars from various fields, including history, economics, politics, and journalism, have written volumes attempting to understand the causes of the worst economic period since the Great Depression. Their analyses reflect how complicated, intertwined, opaque, and impaired our modern global financial system is. I have pulled together several of their conclusions—which are sometimes conflicting—regarding the reasons behind the deep and prolonged economic downturn of the 2010s. When viewed through a mythological lens, images of certain gods come into focus. Perhaps more concerning is that many gods, and more noticeably, various goddesses, are missing from the drama of the GFC.

As discussed earlier, Greece's experience during the crisis will be considered in greater detail as it captured the imagination of many experts who sought to understand how such a small country could be the source of so much commotion. It is worth noting that during the crisis, Greece was known as Europe's problem child (Paganos, 2016, pp. 20–21). However, recently, Greece has become Europe's golden child, earning the title of the *Economist's* Country of the Year 2023. Greece's saga did not end in tragedy.

Experts' Views of the Global Crisis

While experts do not fully agree on all the causes of the crisis, there is broad acceptance that it began in the U.S.: "Ground zero was America's housing market, for sure" (Tooze, 2018, p. 7). The crisis exposed long-standing dysfunctions and corruption within the economic system (e.g., Galbraith, 2016; Roufos, 2018; Tooze, 2018; Varoufakis, 2015). Experts generally agreed that the actions of the investment banks, mortgage companies, the U.S. government, and credit rating agencies played a significant role in the catastrophe. The changes in government legislation in the 1990s allowed mortgage companies to relax lending criteria, encouraging people to take on debt through low interest rates and tax breaks. Individual borrowers took on mortgages

DOI: 10.4324/9781003497622-3

they could not afford, and banks and mortgage companies took on risky loans. The increase in credit stirred the imagination as people sought the American dream of owning their own home, but the increased debt summoned the much-feared goddess, Ananke, and her yoke.

The risk was compounded by the deregulation of the financial sector, which enabled financial institutions to engage in a broader range of activities. Investment banks developed dicey and obscure financial products, some of which contained the dubious mortgages, and sold them to international financial institutions, creating global risk. Financial institutions also took on considerable debt. Excessive credit was carelessly thrown around, and too much debt was rashly taken on. The U.S. government failed to keep a close enough eye on what was happening, and credit rating agencies failed to do their job and call out the higher risk. There was a lot of blame to go around, which was not confined to the United States. The U.K., with more lax regulations, attracted U.S. banks (Tooze, 2018).

Eventually, the financial institutions' bad behavior caught up with them, and deep cracks appeared. House prices fell, and people lost their homes, savings, businesses, and jobs. Financial institutions began to experience significant losses. The money flow froze, the trust stopped, and the people paid the price. The U.S. government stepped up to bail out the failing financial system; "Hundreds of billions of taxpayer funds were put in play to rescue greedy banks" (Tooze, 2018, p. 12). Unpalatable as it is, it appeared to work well enough as the U.S. carried on with life, although not without its victims, usually not the wealthy bankers (p. 12). The book and film *The Big Short* (McKay, 2015) go a long way to untangle and portray financial institutions' complex and fraudulent behavior. Images of the greedy Titans and slippery Hermes fill the screen.

The gods and goddesses in the crisis will be explored throughout the rest of the book, but it is worth noting that the crisis began in the housing market. Houses were looked at first and foremost as commodities rather than as centers for the family and community. Hestia is lost when the housing market has been commoditized, and the health of the family and the community is disregarded. The greed of the business Titans and the irresponsible and tricksterish behavior of the financial institutions leave no space for her; "In society, Titanism is present whenever exploitative motives and mechanistic thinking overtake human and cultural values" (Slater, 2015, p. 3).

In *The Big Short*, Ben Rickert, portrayed by Brad Pitt, seems to be the only one who recognizes this when he chastises his two proteges for celebrating the fortune they will earn when the housing market fails:

> If we're right, people lose homes. People lose jobs. People lose retirement savings; people lose pensions. You know what I hate about fucking banking? It reduces people to numbers. Here's a number—every 1% unemployment goes up, 40,000 people die. Did you know that?

Perhaps the financial difficulties could have been contained if America's financial system was an island, but financial institutions worldwide took on the high-risk financial products, thus exposing themselves to the toxic situation. Many countries also had their own domestic financial challenges; the U.S. was not the only country whose housing market was problematic. The crisis spread worldwide, including in Europe, where the Eurozone leaders did too little too late, causing "tens of millions of its citizens into the depths of a 1930s-style depression" (Tooze, 2018, p. 15). Spain, Cyprus, Greece, Portugal, Italy, and Ireland were particularly impacted and required international help to get their economies back on track.

Experts pointed out that the crisis revealed specific issues within the structure of the European economic system, arguing it was not viable from the start and that the European Monetary Unit was flawed from the beginning (Galbraith, 2016; Kalyvas, 2015; Varoufakis, 2015). Although EU countries have a common currency, they have lost local fiscal sovereignty and policies. Countries cannot address issues with standard economic strategies, such as changing currency exchange rates. There are also inherent differences in countries' economies, with Northern countries generally being stronger and extending credit to the countries of the South who have found themselves as debtors.

In his book, *The Global Minotaur: America, the True Origins of the Financial Crisis and the Future of the World* Economy, Yanis Varoufakis (2015), the controversial ex-finance minister of Greece, argued that the causes of the crisis stemmed back even further, particularly to the 1970s when the gold standard was abandoned, and the global economic system became reliant on the U.S. dollar. He compared the U.S.'s consumption of goods and capital to the ancient Greek monster, the Minotaur, with the head of a bull and the body of a man who required continual sacrifices of young people. Varoufakis blamed the U.S.'s high trade and budget deficits, the greed of Wall Street, and the deregulation of the financial markets for creating the perilous situation. Roufos (2018) argued that the result of financial institutions' changing practices was "new problems related to the increase of public debt and the foundation of economic growth on the expansion of credit" (p. 31). There was a lack of the positive aspects of Saturn as the wise old man in our current financial system and far too much Ananke.

There was also a lack of Themis, the goddess of justice. Mukunda (2018) described the injustices in the handling of the crisis. Despite the U.S. financial sector crippling the global economy, it received little punishment. The leaders were given bailouts to keep their organizations solvent; none of them lost their jobs, and they kept their pay. Unlike GM and Chrysler, when bailed out, the CEOs were fired, and the workforce endured pay cuts. The decisions made by the government "gave the appearance of a government willing to spare no expense to shelter Wall Street from the consequences of its own mistakes, while largely unwilling to make similar efforts for others" (para. 8).

Mukunda (2018) noted that the economic definition of justice is based on efficiency: "The outcome is the one that maximizes welfare" (para. 5). The government argued that bailouts were required to prevent another Great Depression. This feels Apollonian, meaning it was a decision based on ration and lacking emotions or any sense of fairness. Most people see justice as fairness, reflected in the goddess Themis, who is "the blindfolded figure with sword and scales who prides over law courts" (Donleavy & Shearer, 2008, p. 1). Themis was the original leader of the ancient Greek economic world at Delphi, which still plays a significant role in modern-day economics. Apollo murdered Themis's serpent and claimed the oracle for himself. Efficiency trumps fairness.

Greece's Experience of the Crisis

Greece also experienced a lack of fairness in its experience of the crisis, and it suffered greatly. During the worst part of the crisis, nearly one-third of Greeks were unemployed, including youth unemployment rates of 60%. Personal incomes were reduced by a third, and the economy shrank by 25%. To appreciate the desperate situation that Greece was facing, it is worth noting that it was like the experience of the U.S. during the Great Depression (Kalyvas, 2015, p. 174). Greece's precarious situation led to a fear of "Grexit," that Greece would leave the euro, and the European currency would be discredited (p. 174). Ultimately, Greece had to be bailed out by a group of international lenders, which resulted in "the most expensive financial rescue of a country ever" (p. 3).

Perhaps even more troubling was the number of young Greeks who left the country for a better future elsewhere. Young people could not afford to get married or have children; birth rates fell to 1.3 children per family (Brabant, 2017). Sotiris Xtouris, a Greek professor of sociology, called this exodus "the annihilation of a generation" (para. 20). Galbraith (2016) created a clear image of the suffering; "The stress of daily life in Greece since 2010 has been enormous, and the country has been marked by rising rates of homelessness, emigration, and suicide—the social and psychological markers of economic failure" (p. 4).

Along with dealing with fiscal issues, Greece also had to endure the worst of Europe's refugee crisis as one of the main landing places for people seeking sanctuary from the war-torn countries of Syria, Iraq, and Afghanistan. In 2010, Greece accounted for "90 percent of all detections of illegal border crossings into the EU", and the number of crossings multiplied during the crisis (Palaiologos, 2015, p. 198). Regulations stipulated that asylum seekers must apply from their first point of entry, which put tremendous pressure on Greece which put tremendous pressure on the Greek asylum processing system (p. 197).

Causes of the Greek Crisis

Greece's situation caught the attention of many experts, who explored the crisis and created images of Greece's plight in their books: *The 13th Labour of Hercules* (Palaiologos, 2015), *The Full Catastrophe: Travels Among the New Greek Ruins* (Angelos, 2016), *A Happy Future is a Thing of the Past* (Roufos, 2018), *Welcome to the Poisoned Chalice* (Galbraith, 2016), and *Crucible of Resistance* (Laskos & Tsakalotos, 2013).

The experts' opinions about the causes of the Greek crisis varied and, in some cases, differed significantly. It is important to note that the dysfunctions identified by the experts as problematic in Greece are not unique to Greece. Many nations experience the same dysfunctions, which undermine economic health. For example, scholars pointed out the Greek government's corruption, greed, and irresponsibility; however, as can be seen clearly in the GFC, Greece does not hold a monopoly on those. There is a reason for delving into the details of Greece, which will become apparent in the following chapters. For instance, some of the critiques of Greek culture highlight unhealed collective trauma.

Most experts acknowledged issues external to Greece, such as the above-mentioned problems with the Eurozone and global capitalism. Nearly all the experts criticized the Troika, consisting of the International Monetary Fund, European Central Bank, and the European Union, under the leadership of the German Chancellor, Angela Merkel, for their harsh bail-out terms. Many experts also noted internal issues in Greece, idiosyncracies of Greek culture, such as tax evasion and the close relationship between church and state. A Greek hotel owner summed it up well; "'First, Greece has the problem of itself. Second, Greece has the problem of the Troika'" (Angelos, 2016, p. 17). Despite much doom and gloom, most experts recognized the Greek people's incredible intelligence, resourcefulness, and resilience and held hope that Greece would emerge from the crisis alive and well.

External Issues

Most experts noted the misdeeds of the European governments and banks that were rescued and de-risked at Greece's expense;

> When the world financial crisis hit, it was no surprise that European banks would dump risk—in the form of peripheral country debts…Nor was it any surprise that the governments placed rescue of their own banks far above any concern for the consequences of Greece.
>
> (Galbraith, 2016, p. 3)

Almost all the experts criticized the Troika for being overly harsh. Kuper (2017) referred to Greece as "the eurozone's body in the cupboard, sacrificed to save the euro" (para. 6). The Troika was aware that Greece could not repay its debts. Yet, they did not restructure or reduce them because they wanted to avoid losses for their banks (Galbraith, 2016). They also disregarded human aspects, including investment strategies appropriate to the local culture and the need for education and employment. The Troika failed to consider that most Greek businesses were small firms, and when banks tightened their lending, businesses struggled without access to liquidity (Kalyvas, 2015).

The bail-out loans required Greece to agree to severe austerity measures and implement significant changes, including raising taxes, curbing tax evasion, and cutting budgets and pensions. Galbraith (2016) argued that the bail-out requirements did nothing for Greece's growth and long-term prospects. Instead, they reinforced the power and financial stability of France and Germany, "who cannot accept that the lender is anything other than the offended party" (p. 33).

Galbraith (2015) expressed concern that Greece's ultimate outcome would likely result in the emigration of its professional population and a foreign takeover of its banking systems, real estate, and marketable assets, potentially turning into something akin to "a Caribbean dependency of the United States" (p. 19). Similarly, Beaton (2019) contended that Greece had become a debt colony, describing it as "Europe's symbolic colonization of Greece" (p. 388). Laskos and Tsakalotos (2013) also highlighted the significant increase in debt and decrease in savings for both Greek individuals and the government following Greece's adoption of the euro, as Greek businesses and financiers focused on short-term profits and inexpensive money (p. 40).

Despite all the criticisms of the Troika, Angelos (2016) also argued that they were successful in some respects. First and foremost, Greece did not go bankrupt, which could have easily happened. Greece also reduced its fiscal deficit, made its public-sector employment more reasonable, and controlled its spending.

Internal Factors

Regarding "the problem of itself," experts argued that significant problems within the Greek government and idiosyncracies within the Greek culture contributed to the crisis. Discussing a nation's culture is difficult as culture is neither homogenous nor stagnant. However, the experts concentrated on prevalent, long-standing, challenging elements of Greek culture and institutions. However, the experts disagreed about their impact. Laskos and Tsakalotos (2013) contended that the problems of Greece paled in comparison to the issues of the EU and capitalism, describing them as "nuggets of truth swamped in a sea of distortion and blind spots" (p. 33). Others argued they contributed meaningfully to Greece's precarious position even before the crisis.

Some experts noted that Greece has endured a series of crises in its modern history and seems to "stumble from disaster to disaster" (Kalyvas, 2015, p. 13). The experts also noted the corruption and inefficiencies of the

Greek government. In a 2013 survey, Greece's government was ranked in the lowest position in the EU and 80th globally in perceptions of corruption (Kalyvas, 2015, p. 169). Nepotism was a significant problem, and interest groups highly influenced the government, undermining the democratic processes and exchanging favors for votes. The government was run by clientelism, and individuals' ties to political parties were crucial to accomplishing anything. The experts also identified business and public-sector corruption. People get things done through fakelakia, which means small envelope and is Greek slang for bribery (Angelos, 2016; Palaiologos, 2015).

Before the crisis, the Greek government spent recklessly, particularly on public-sector jobs and pensions, while neglecting to collect taxes, including from wealthy shipping magnates. This led to an explosion of debt (Angelos, 2016; Kalyvas, 2015; Palaiologos, 2015). A report by Rabobank (Wijffelaars & Loman, 2015) noted that much of Greece's borrowed money went toward consumption, such as high public spending, rather than fiscally responsible investment.

Greece scored well below average in the *Index of Economic Freedom*, which found that Greece is considered "mostly unfree" due to its laws, regulatory inefficiencies, and government interference (Verouchi, 2015, p. 22). Greek legal regulations hindered foreign investment (Palaiologos, 2015, p. 137) and negatively impacted entrepreneurship, private investment, and growth (Kalyvas, 2015, p. 138). In its annual Doing Business Report 2019, the World Bank found that Greece's scores in the "Ease of Doing Business" category have declined, leaving Greece ranked 72nd globally (World Bank, 2019). Greece's "statist crony capitalism" meant the old rule kept down the young entrepreneurs (Palaiologos, p. 222). Saturn eats his children.

The World Bank Report (2019) ranked Greece 135 out of 140 countries in the "Future Orientation of Government" category, citing that the Greek government does not have a clear direction or a plan to move toward the future. Greece has issues in its ability to respond to changes, lacks political stability and a long-term vision, and has been slow to adapt to technological changes. The innovative Hermes is absent.

But negative Hermes abounds in the government's overall lack of accountability: "Underlying it all, there is a pervasive irresponsibility, a sense that no one is in charge, no one is willing or able to act as a custodian of the common good that government is meant to represent" (Palaiologos, 2015, p. xi). Roufos (2018) outlined how none of the governments in power during the crisis could do the right thing by Greece and negotiate reasonable terms with the Troika.

In Greek culture, there is a tendency to blame others and avoid responsibility. The Greeks are adept at the game of *ballaki euthinon,* or "little ball of blame," with the goal of: "When responsibility for a disaster in question heads your way, you do your best to flick it as far away as possible, preferably by directing it towards some other murkily involved party" (Palaiologos, 2015, p. x).

Greece is not the only nation proficient at this game; it would make for an interesting World Series.

Scholars have argued that some of the Greek population tends to be conspiracy-minded, anti-capitalist, anti-American, and anti-European. Verouchi (2015) noted that Greeks often believe their sufferings stem from other Western nations' "envy" of their ancient contributions to the world (p. 15). The resistance to a rules-based domineering government seems to have become ingrained in the psyche of the Greek people and is seen in the 20,000 strikes and protests during the financial crisis (Angelos, 2016; Palaiologos, 2015; Verouchi, 2015). Palaiologos (2015) noted that the Greek people feel burdened with fixing the corrupt behavior of the ruling elite, which certainly has its merits.

The Greek people blamed the corrupt politicians for "eating" all the money despite widespread tax evasion (Angelos, 2016; Palaiologos, 2015; Verouchi, 2015). Tax evasion is not considered deviant behavior in Greece but rather the usual way of doing business (Palaiologos, 2015, p. 28). This is particularly true for people who could avoid recording their income, including many professions such as doctors, lawyers, and politicians. A study from 2012 found there was approximately 11.2 billion euros of uncollected tax revenue, which contributed to Greece's economic problems (p. 29).

Kalyvas (2015) noted a paradox in Greek culture: the structure of the economy is collectivist, but in spirit, it is "every man for himself" (p. 140). Verouchi (2015) also noticed this; "Greeks seem to have no knowledge of their responsibilities towards their country and their compatriots as part of their social contract" (p. 14). This is also clearly seen in many other countries, including the U.S. culture, which will be explored in Chapter 6.

The scholars also pointed out the impact of Greece's fractured politics on its economy, which was made worse by the actions of the Troika and their own Government (Angelos, 2016; Kalyvas, 2015; Palaiologos, 2015; Verouchi, 2015). Greece's political parties reside in various places on the political continuum, including a far-right party and a far-left communist party. Kalyvas argued that the unsettled political situation and bickering between the parties significantly slowed the reform process.

There appear to be two conflicting archetypal underpinnings in Greek culture: the "Helleno-Romaic" struggle between a "cosmopolitan, Western-leaning, modern worldview on the one hand, and an Orthodox, Eastern-leaning, traditionalist sensibility on the other" (Kalyvas, 2015, pp. 7–8). Greece also oscillates between self-aggrandizement and "a sense of insecurity and a feeling of persecution" (p. 5), which leads it to, ultimately, a need to be constantly defensive.

So, Greece appears split in various ways: in politics and geography, between the people and the government, and between Greece and the rest of Europe and the world. The Greeks also appear conflicted in their history; they have a "complicated relationship with their ancient past" (Palaiologos, 2015, p. xviii), which will be discussed further in the next chapter.

Many experts noted the significant influence of the Greek Orthodox Church on Greek culture and its negative influence on economic development. There is no separation of church and state in Greece, as the Greek War of Independence from the Ottoman Empire "cemented" the association (Kalyvas, 2015, p. 42). The Orthodox Church plays a prominent role in the lives of the Greeks and "sees itself as the torchbearer of Hellenism through the ages, and the guardian of Greek identity" (Angelos, 2016, p. 160). The Church may have contributed to the economic crisis as it is against modernization and acts "not always in the service of stability and almost never in the cause of social progress" (Palaiologos, 2015, p. 16). George Prokopiou, a billionaire Greek shipowner, sees the Greek attitude as the problem "'we want businesses to invest and to pay taxes, but we don't want the businessman. We still think of profit as sinful, we cultivate envy. If that does not change, things will not improve'" (p. 189).

The experts identified steps that Greece needs to take, including creating a development strategy that should "paint a picture of an attractive and viable future" and "it needs a vision, around which the Greek people can converge" (Galbraith, 2016, p. 89). The wisdom of the imagination is required. Angelos (2016) argued against Greece's financial colonialism and for stability and fairness in Greece's future rather than focusing on competition and wealth.

Although the authors criticize the Greek government and culture for contributing to the crisis, some also point out the positive contributions. Kalyvas (2015) argued that Greece is a trailblazer and reminded us that Greece is new to the modern world and one of the first non-Western countries to attempt to westernize (p. 2). The significance of this is not to be underestimated. He argued that Greece could be seen as a success story as, despite the number of military coups, wars, and dictatorships it has dealt with over the last century, it has become a part of the world's most successful democracies and one of the most prosperous countries in the region.

Angelos (2016) also recognized that the crisis was a time of opportunity for Greece to transform itself into something more socially just and economically self-sufficient. Verouchi (2015) argued that Greece has potential in its people and their ideas and geographical location (p. 53). Kuper (2017) noted how vital the Greek family was in the crisis; "most people are saved by the Greek family, the eternal safety net in a nation with a weak state" (para. 9). Hestia is still there somewhere.

Greece appears to have been in chaos during the Global Financial Crisis; however, depth psychology recognizes that chaos is the void from which the gods originated (Kershaw, 2007). From turmoil, new ways of being can emerge.

Digging Deeper: Uncovering Archetypal Roots

After reading the experts' explorations, I was left feeling somewhat unsatisfied, as if something had not been uncovered and the crux had not quite been found. It also became clear that the issues in Greece were dysfunctions found in most capitalistic societies. What nation is innocent of the rich evading taxes, government corruption and inefficiencies, and a tendency to blame the "other"? It was as if Greece aimed to reveal the fundamental problems within the global economic system. As I continued to follow Greece's red thread, it led me to consider the role of place in economic health.

References

Angelos, J. (2016). *The full catastrophe: Travels among the new Greek ruins*. Broadway Books.

Beaton, R. (2019). *Greece: Biography of a modern nation*. Allen Lane.

Brabant, M. (Correspondent). (2017, November 13). *PBS News Hour* [Television transcript]. Greece: Public Broadcasting Service. Retrieved from https://www.pbs.org/newshour/show/brain-drain-and-declining-birth-rate-threaten-the-future-of-greece

Donleavy, P., & Shearer, A. (2008). *From ancient myth to modern healing: Themis: Goddess of heart-soul, justice and reconciliation*. Routledge.

Galbraith, J. K. (2016). *Welcome to the poisoned chalice: The destruction of Greece and the future of Europe*. Yale University Press.

Kalyvas, S. N. (2015). *Modern Greece: What everyone needs to know*. Oxford University Press.

Kershaw, S. P. (2007). *The Greek myths: Gods, monsters, heroes and the origins of storytelling*. Robinson.

Kuper, S. (2017, July 8/9). How the Greeks have adjusted to the forever crisis. *The Financial Times*.

Laskos, C., & Tsakalotos, E. (2013). *Crucible of resistance: Greece, the Eurozone & the economic crisis*. Pluto Press.

McKay, A. (Director). (2015). *The big short* [Film]. Paramount Pictures.

Mukunda, G. (2018, September 25). The social and political costs of the financial crisis, 10 years later. *Harvard Business Review*. Retrieved from https://hbr.org/2018/09/the-social-and-political-costs-of-the-financial-crisis-10-years-later

Paganos, S. M. (2016, May June). My big fat Greek debt. *Athens insider: The art of Athens*, *15*(127), 20–21.

Palaiologos, Y. (2015). *The 13th labour of Hercules: Inside the Greek crisis*. Portobello Books.

Roufos, P. (2018). *A happy future is a thing of the past: The Greek crisis and other disasters*. Reaktion.

Slater, G. (2015). *Finding the Gods in a titanic age*. Arquetípica. www.arquetipica.com.br.

Tooze, A. (2018). *Crashed: How a decade of financial crises changed the world*. Penguin.

Varoufakis, Y. (2015). *The global Minotaur: America, Europe and the future of the global economy*. CPI.

Verouchi, V. (2015). *Cultural barriers to prosperity: The case of Greece* [Working Paper]. Retrieved from The Fletcher School Tufts University: https://sites.tufts.edu/karamanlischair/files/2018/12/Karamanlis-Working-Papers-2015-No-3.pdf

Wijffelaars, M., & Loman, H. (2015). *The eurozone (debt) crisis-causes and crisis response*. Retrieved from Rabobank website: https://economics.rabobank.com/publications/2015/december/the-eurozone-debt-crisis--causes-and-crisis-response/

World Bank Group. (2019). *Doing business* 2019*: Training for reform*. Retrieved from https://www.worldbank.org/content/dam/doingBusiness/media/Annual-Reports/English/DB2019-report_web-version.pdf

4 A Depth Psychological View of Place and Economics

The worldwide impact of the Global Financial Crisis served as a stark reminder that no country is a metaphorical island, even if it is a literal one. We all inhabit the same planet, and our actions are not confined by our nation's borders. The crisis also showed how economics, *oikonomia*, moved away from its original associations with the household, the land, and the people, finding itself firmly in the bank accounts of the business Titans. Building on the insights of Hyun Song Shin, one of the foremost thinkers in finance, Tooze (2018) argued, "We need to analyze the global economy not in terms of an 'island model' of international economic interaction—national economy to national economy—but through the 'interlocking matrix' of corporate balance sheets—bank to bank" (p. 9). Perhaps cutting ties to the gold standard in 1971 was symbolic of economics' conclusive division from the riches and grounding of the Earth.

From a depth psychological perspective, the dislocation of economics from the Earth, the places people reside, and the people themselves is problematic. Jung (Sabini, 2002) wrote extensively about the detrimental impact of Western culture's neglect of Nature, both the environment and the natural, instinctual aspects of human nature. As mentioned earlier, one of the principles of depth psychology is that people are deeply connected to an ensouled world, the anima mundi (Coppin & Nelson, 2005). Depth psychology's systemic approach recognizes that no aspect of our socioeconomic or psychological lives can be experienced in isolation. People's health, the environment, and economics are eternally intertwined.

Depth psychology digs into the cultural unconscious, or the "fundamental psychological roots" that prohibit an honoring of Nature (Kiehl, 2016, p. xii). One of the strongest, thickest roots lies in Western culture's Cartesian Christian perspective. The self and the world are divided into subject and object, with people striving to dominate what they perceive as an unintelligent nature (Tarnas, 2013). The Christian principles impacting our relationship with money also distort our connection to Nature; the belief that man is made in the image of God adds to the idea that humans are superior to Nature (Tarnas, 2013). Jung understood the divinity of Nature, arguing that Nature is matter and spirit.

DOI: 10.4324/9781003497622-4

A depth psychological view of the role of places and the environment in economic health would address some of the concerns of countercultural movements within economics and expand economic success beyond growing GDPs. Depth psychology values places beyond their natural resources and auspicious geographical locations and considers a holistic view of cultural and environmental health.

A Depth Psychological View of Place

Where people live impacts everything about them; "the place we occupy, however briefly—has everything to do with what and who we are (and finally, *that* we are)" (Casey, 2009, p. xiii). People cannot exist without a place. Places enable people's cultural and economic lives. Casey argued that Western culture disregards place in the interest of time, even though places are needed for time to present itself. This perspective prioritizes Father Time, embodied in the god Saturn, over Mother Earth, the goddess Themis. The earthly feminine soul-life loses out again to the spiritual masculine.

Depth psychology defines place beyond physical location and geography to encompass everything about the locale and the people, including the spiritual, physical, cultural, and psychological. Each place has a unique essence and may hold specific archetypal energies:

> Place transcends the usual divides between natural and cultural, urban and wild, sacred and profane. Their interwoven textures embody habitat, climate, geology, history, memory, story and language, jurisdiction, economic use, etc. and also the spiritus loci (spirit of the place).
>
> (Hillman, 2006, p. 334)

In Western culture, "God-given" nature is often seen as soulful and good, while cities are perceived as corrupt and evil (Hillman, 2006, p. 292). However, a deep connection exists between city and soul. Cities are a place for soul; "How we imagine our cities, how we envision their goals and values and enhance their beauty defines the self of each person in that city, for the city is the solid exhibition of the communal soul" (p. 115).

Places are living organisms with individual souls interacting with the beings who dwell there; "the geological, geographical, and ecological forces that constitute our physical world also enact themselves within our psychic life" (Chalquist & Barnwell, 2023, p. 4). How we care for the world, including the places we live, impacts our psychological lives (Hillman, 2006). To find the communal soul, we must look beyond the churches and spiritual centers and into the people's day-to-day lives, such as the shops and bars, sports teams, and shadowy alleyways (Hillman). A community's soul is also experienced in the art that the city commissions and in the graffiti that appears in the dark of night. Soul is felt in how a place is cared for or neglected. Places hold our emotional memories, collective traumas, and our connections to the ancestors. Disregarding place is a neglect of the soul and our psychological lives. Thus, we cannot evaluate economic health and development without considering place.

Changing our approach to economics requires us to change our worldview. Along with reenchanting Nature, we must collaborate with it rather than try to dominate it. By doing so, we can help in the co-evolution of the world and act as "an organ of the universe's self-revelation" (Tarnas, 2013, p. 21). We must also honor a place's genius loci—its guardian spirit and natural essence. We must listen to the Earth and its inhabitants because they hold the wisdom to evolve our culture and raise consciousness. Terrapsychology provides ways to do so.

Terrapsychology

Before I knew anything about the theory and research methodology of terrapsychology, I experienced it in Greece. The words "It's not what you look at that matters; it's what you see" were etched on the door of my Athens hotel. Henry David Thoreau's revised quote captured how I learned to engage with Greece: I approached it through a metaphorical and symbolic lens and endeavored to listen to Greece's soul.

I was not the only one who approached Greece this way. While walking around the sacred grounds of Eleusis, the site of the ancient religious rites dedicated to the goddesses Demeter and Persephone, I encountered a group of people making a documentary (Degnan Smith, 2023). Instead of filming Eleusis, they placed a microphone in the ear-shaped Plutonian cave where Persephone purportedly traveled to the Underworld and became its Queen. They wanted to listen to the Underworld. Mythologically, the Underworld symbolizes the realm of the unconscious and soul. They, like me, seemed to be listening for its wisdom.

I stumbled upon terrapsychology during my research process. Craig Chalquist developed terrapsychology by extending and integrating concepts from depth psychology, ecopsychology, and systems theory. Terrapsychology seeks to reenchant the world and recognizes that people and the places they dwell influence and reflect each other; "the region in which you live also lives inside of you" (Chalquist & Barnwell, 2023, p. 1). Viewing places through a terrapsychological lens facilitates a view of a place's soul because terrapsychology "pays attention to the stories, myths, legends, and symbols that occur within an environment by studying and feeling into the intelligible patterns of an environment's genius loci" (p. 9).

By engaging with places symbolically, we can ascertain their archetypal patterns and the psyches of their inhabitants. By exploring a place's images—such as its landscapes and the condition of its roads and rivers—we can glimpse its natural essence and understand the state of the collective psyche of its people. Chalquist and Barnwell (2023) pose the questions, "What if the anima mundi is calling out to us through the symbols that it presents to us in the world? What shifts would take place if we interpreted the physicality of the world like we would a dream?" (p. 4). What shifts would occur in economics if we listened to the Earth and its places? What shifts would occur in economics if we honored a place's genius loci?

Terrapsychology also advocates for collaboration with the anima mundi: "The ensouled world calls upon us to co-create ideas and practices that reenchant and inspire" (Chalquist & Barnwell, 2023, p. 5). A terrapsychological approach also helps uncover obstacles to a community's economic health by revealing the shadows within a place's culture that influence its inhabitants' behavior. It informs us about the psychological state of the inhabitants. A place's images reveal what ails it, which is critical because unhealed wounds in the collective psyche cause behaviors that are counterproductive to psychological, environmental, and economic health. A terrapsychological view of the Global Financial Crisis reveals many open wounds, which will be explored throughout the book. It also highlights the archetypes at play in some places central to the crisis.

A Terrapsychological View of the Global Financial Crisis

Tooze's (2018) analysis of the Global Financial Crisis reflected how money is not only disconnected from animals, Nature, deities, and even human leaders but also no longer tied to places, including nations; "what drives global trade are not the relationships between national economies but multinational corporations coordinating far-flung 'value chains'" (p. 8). Modern-day money has lost all grounding, finding itself in big business's balance sheets in the cloud.

When looked at mythologically, we find ourselves back with Saturn and the Titans, which "represented the raw, undifferentiated drive for power and domination through mere strength and size" (Slater, 2024, p. 375). The Titans were not subject to any laws, a bit like the leaders of the finance industry who suffered little punishment for their misdeeds in the crisis.

The ancient Greeks knew it took the Olympic gods and goddesses, who were deeply connected to Nature, to disempower the Titans and imprison them under the sea. In modern times, the way to counter the Titanic forces in our culture is by tending to the archetypal energies that the gods and goddesses represent (Slater, 2024). For instance, the emotional life of Dionysus, the beauty of Aphrodite, Hestia's care of the hearth and home, and the father-like Zeus help to submerge the drive for power and control.

As mentioned earlier, the image of the origins of the GFC in the housing market reflects a neglected Hestia, the goddess strongly associated with place and home. The government may have relaxed lending criteria to help marginalized communities afford housing, but the financial institutions took advantage of the situation. Rather than honoring family and community, homes became commodities, and Hermes, the trickster and thief, was more present than Hestia, who was the center of the home and community and the most upright and charitable (Paris, 1986, p. 167). Ecological problems are part of the consequence of ignoring Hestia as the world around us deteriorates (Paris).

Hestia's image is the flame and the hearth. She is the goddess of places, including communities and nations; "She signifies the sacredness of being centered, rooted, and contained in a collective group and in a particular region, a local soil" (Edinger, 1994, p. 40). She is the "center of the Earth, the center of the home, and our own personal center" (Paris, p. 167). The loss of Hestia contributes to the loss of family and community. Terrapsychology's ambition to reenchant brings Hestia back to Earth and home; "In challenging the human-centered myth of humans as separate from the world around us, we then seek to transcend the ongoing objectification and commodification of life on this Earth" (Chalquist & Barnwell, 2023, p. 4).

The dominance of the sky father, Saturn, also reflects the neglect of the powerful Earth Mother, embodied in the goddess Themis, who was "hailed as the incarnation of the eternal, inexhaustible Earth herself, and she brings an ancient wisdom to their ordering of the world of gods and humans" (Donleavy & Shearer, 2008, p. 1). She brought people together in social assembly, and her "very name means an ancient, divine law, a right order established by nature itself for the living together of gods and humans" (p. 1).

Themis strives to rebalance when things are neglected, helping to alleviate conflict by embracing natural differences. Themis may very well represent the archetype of the Self in all its complexities and wholeness (Donleavy & Shearer, 2008, p. 5). An approach to economics whose values reflect Themis's call for cohesion, peace, Earth, and justice looks very different from the one that Apollo and the Titans rule today. This is particularly clear in a terrapsychological view of Manhattan.

A Terrapsychological View of Manhattan

Taking a terrapsychological view of the roots of the GFC takes us to the peaks of Manhattan's skyscrapers, particularly those on Wall Street whose cement and glass structures, like the financier's profits, continue to reach new heights. The U.S. is, after all, perceived to be the land of endless riches. Manhattan's genius loci seems to have archetypal connections to markets and influence. When NYC was populated by the real native New Yorkers, the Lenape people, a park on Wall Street, Bowling Green, was a place of power and a "sacred spot where council fires were held, and great orators came to speak from time to time" (Pritchard, 2002, p. 65). It was also a place of trade. However, the Lenape's approach to power and markets differed greatly from today's Wall Street financiers. The Lenape people cared for the Earth and their fellow people; "At one time the land and the people of New York were one. The timeless harmony with nature and neighbor known to the northernmost Algonquin today was also known to the original people of New York City" (p. 2). Despite a high population density, the land was pristine and well-tended.

The Lenape were kind, intelligent, mild, and affectionate (Pritchard, 2002, p. 47). They held a systemic view of the world and respected suffering and feelings, true diversity, and limitations and strengths (p. 16). Their worldview seems to hold Themis and Hestia in deep regard as their message was: "Honor the earth. We belong to our mother, and without her we are lost" (p. 16). The "Grandfathers, the elder statesmen of the realm" who were wise peacemakers (p. 47), would be very disappointed in today's business Titans, or the "dark fathers" (p. 54).

The Lenape's wampum beads became the legal tender of the new world; "It was a combination of the Lenape skill and speed in creating wampum and Dutch marketing ingenuity that created the basis for a 'free world economy' near Wall Street" (Pritchard, 2002, p. 130). The wampum originally had sacred ties; they were works of art "used as visual aids in sacred story-telling ceremonies in which the history of the people was recounted in full" (p. 130). Thus, the wampum helped keep the people connected to their past and ancestors.

In 1653, the Dutch built a wall at the site of today's Wall Street to keep the Lenape from the places of trade and power (Pritchard, 2002, p. 65). Wall Street was a physical manifestation of how the colonialized world cut off the Lenape—"the keepers of the sacred land" (p. 53)—and their worldview from the powers of finance and economics. The Lenape compared the Dutch to the story of the two-colored snake who, the more it is fed, the bigger its appetite until it becomes a monster and "begins devouring the land and everything on it" (p. 137).

New York's namesake, York, England, is the place of the wild boar, which was often the cause of the hero's downfall in mythology. The woman-boar sat at the crossroads and avenged the mistreatment of women, animals, and Mother Earth; "That's New York in a nutshell, the place at the crossroads where the strongest and most heroic are tempted and destroyed by the seductive attractions of earthly life" (Pritchard, 2002, p. 19). Jung believed there is frequently a reckoning when an element of the psyche or culture has been ignored or ill-treated. Perhaps the woman-boar will have her vengeance.

Manhattan seems to hold archetypes of the dark, hardened, unfeeling father and the underworld (Pritchard, 2002). These reflect elements of a cold, hardened Saturn, also called the senex. Pritchard calls Manhattan the "city with amnesia" because it is a city of immigrants without a long-standing history in the place, because it has walled out the Lenape people's deep roots (p. 17). Manhattan's tall buildings and fast and future-focused movements bring in the archetype of the puer, often seen in Hermes. The senex and puer are an archetypal duo of the old man and the eternal child who are frequently found at the source of cultural challenges, including those in Greece during the crisis.

A Terrapsychological View of Greece

When one thinks of Greece, images of glorious beaches, pristine waters, friendly people, delicious food, and grand ancient sites usually spring to mind. Aphrodite, the goddess of love, beauty, and desire, and Dionysus, the god of wine, pleasure, and much more, are clearly at play in the southernmost country in Europe and its thousands of islands scattered across various seas. However, many visitors are surprised by its capital, Athens, which "can repel with its great stretches of concrete and cement, its mass, its fumes and noises of motorcars and klaxons" (Llewelyn Smith, 2004, p. 2). But, as Llewelyn Smith also noted, Athens fascinates.

Greece is more than just beaches and sunshine; two-thirds of the country is covered by mountains, which can be snow-covered. It lies at the crossroads of East and West. Greece is complex and conflicting, a quality that was apparent even in ancient times:

> The natural divisions of the Greek landscape by large mountain masses, arduous pathways and countless islands encouraged the organization of the population into small autonomous regions characterized by an urban centre and the eventual emergence of the city-state (polis)- the predominant political structure of ancient Greece. Despite shared traditions and customs, the city-states' differences were crucial and their individual interests so in opposition that they often gave rise to conflicts and wars.
>
> (Kouveli, Dollis, & Leonard, 2017, p. 12)

Perhaps the natural landscape of Greece required the ancient people to honor Themis, who could contain and find order in the differences and conflict. She holds diversity without insisting on homogeneity.

There is also complexity and conflict in modern-day Greece's built places; "Athens is a city of neighbourhoods, not necessarily distinguished by different architecture or planning, but each with its own character owing something to the origins of the migrants who settled there—for Athens is a city of immigrants" (Llewelyn Smith, 2004, p. 11). Athens and Manhattan have something in common. Athens does not represent all of Greece, just as Manhattan does not reflect the entire U.S. However, Athens, like Manhattan, is Greece's government and financial center. Some might argue that this is the problem with economics: it focuses on the urban at the expense of all else.

During the crisis, many Greek people seemed to wear their hearts on the streets and walls of Athens. Beyond the beauty and activity of the Acropolis was a sense of *kenopsia* in the unkempt public areas, broken pavements, and a glut of abandoned, deteriorating buildings. The empty, half-built homes gave one a sense that there has been a giving up, an acquiescence, a deep depressiveness. Prolific street art expressed grief and rage, as did the tens of thousands of strikes and protests that took place often in Syntagma Square, which houses the Parliament building, prestigious hotels, and luxury shopping. The loss of Hestia was scrawled in graffiti on a wall near the Acropolis; "Our cities turn into commodities."

When I paid attention to the images around Athens, it became clear that this was not Greece's first experience of suffering. It was as if the ghosts of the Greek people's unhealed wounds rose during the crisis. Everywhere I turned, I saw signs of Greece's traumatic past in graffiti, museum exhibitions, art, and cultural activities. Three particular wounds were laid bare: the 400-year Ottoman rule, the German occupation during WWII, and the government dictatorship of the 1970s.

Greece's tensions with Turkey are very much alive today, as are the memories of the Ottoman rule, which threatened to obliterate any signs of a Greek nation, leaving the Greeks to fight for freedom or death. Many Greek scholars recognized its long-lasting impact on Greece and argued it divided Greece in time. Athens is either ancient or modern (post-1820s), with little in between; thus, modern Greece is not just an offshoot of ancient Greece (Beaton, 2019). The Ottoman rule severed modern Greece from its glorious past and its sense of self (Tsempelis, 2016). The violence seemed to split modern Greece into modernizers and traditionalists. The modernizers were "political, statist, pragmatic and integrationist," and the traditionalists were "nostalgic for the absolute freedom celebrated in the songs of the klefts and the brief moments of glorious self-sufficiency enjoyed by some of the warlords of the Revolution" (Beaton, 2019, p. 90). Interestingly, the Greek drachma, often referred to as the world's oldest currency, was reintroduced after the Revolution; before that, it had not been minted for over 17 centuries (p. 6). The reborn drachma was engraved with the image of the Phoenix, like Greece, rising from the ashes.

The Greeks also suffered during World War II under the German occupation. Nearly 800,000 Greek people died, including 300,000 people starving to death. There were also major conflicts within Greece. Memories of Germany's maltreatment of the Greek people were resurrected during the GFC, particularly because German leaders led the bail-out and austerity demands. The Greek media often made Nazi references, and various cultural displays about World War II appeared around Athens. A photographic exhibit at the Ancient Agora (Ministry of Culture, 2018–2019) showed the Nazi's propaganda through the photographs of a German soldier. A more personal account of the war's impact appeared in a documentary about a Greek man whose childhood years before World War II were spent on land filled with fruit orchards. Post-war, the orchards were gone, and he struggled to make a living recycling the broken washing machines and rusting cars that covered that land (Benaki Museum, 2019). This image of the land pre- and post-war seems symbolic of the impact of the war on the psyche of the people.

A third trauma occurred in 1973 at the Athens Polytechnic, where several people were killed during an uprising against the dictatorship government.

This time of dictatorship significantly contributed to forming Greece's national identity. The image of a military tank pushing down the university gates to quell the protesters is deeply embedded in the cultural psyche, seen as the "spectacle of the nation's armed forces being turned against its own youth" (Beaton, 2019, p. 337). Images of the dynamic senex and puer appear again. These wounds are still seen in Athens' anarchist neighborhood, which is rich with cultural life and spectacular street art and a no-go place for police.

The painful situations from Greece's modern history reflect Kalsched's (2013) definition of trauma as "unbearable pain—in other words, affect that cannot be metabolized by the psyche's normal symbolic process" (p. 132). Trauma occurs when we are faced with more than we can bear, resulting in a loss of the capacity to feel and imagine. The psychic fractures caused by trauma are experienced in the physical body, often causing the person to split from the body, and the soul struggles to manifest. Athens's body felt fractured with its broken and chaotic streets. Greece's natural diversity and splinteredness may have been exacerbated by all the trauma the country has endured over many years. As discussed earlier, these wounds often result in complexes, both individual and cultural. Rasche (2016) called cumulative traumas, which are frequently unspoken and passed on through the generations, "crypts in the ego" (p. 28). They sit heavily in the people's souls and are potential earthquakes ready to crack open.

Greece's painful experiences seem to be reflected in its architecture, a consequence of the construction boom driven by economic challenges following World War II. Many lovely old homes were destroyed, and green spaces, including ancient sacred sites, were replaced with apartment buildings. Llewelyn Smith (2004) cited the remarks of Patrick Leigh Fermor, a British author who served in World War II, regarding his observations of Athenians during that period:

> The fever of demolition and rebuilding has the Athenians by the throat. Streets gape as though bombed, masonry crashes, the dust of a siege floats in the air and the clatter of pneumatic drills has replaced the little owl's note as the city's leitmotiv. Rusting whiskers of reinforced concrete prong the sky-line: new hotels soar from the rubble like ogres' mouth-organs. Athens is in a state of headlong flux.
>
> (p. 39)

It is as if the scars from the war became embedded in the streets and homes. They may also have been entrenched in Greece's economic system. According to a report by the European Bank for Reconstruction and Development (Milatovic & Sanfey, 2015), "Greece has the least diversified economy among all EU countries" (para. 3) and "is the least industrialized country in continental EU (except for Luxembourg)" (para. 5). Greece's small manufacturing sector is related to the Earth: food, petroleum, and basic metals processing. Perhaps

Greece's lag in industrialization is due to its difficult history, or perhaps there is something about Greece's genius loci that is not fully aligned with the way Western society has industrialized.

Greece has faced foreign invaders for centuries, and this trend seems to persist in the form of tourism. Economists argued that "Tourism represents the most reliable driver of growth for the Greek economy" (Milatovic & Sanfey, 2015, para. 6). Greece is known for its hospitality and philoxenia, love of strangers, but it seems to be taken to an extreme in the monetization of Hestia; "Renting and operating of real estate is the largest subsector within the real estate activities" (para. 7). Like many other major cities in Europe, short-term rentals contribute to the housing shortage for local people. The Greek people's frustration is seen in the graffiti "Airbnb Tourists F*** off, Refugees welcome." Today's tourism has become a form of invasion, where people ignore a place's soul in their search for the perfect selfie opportunity.

Terrapsychological Excavations

Taking a terrapsychological view of the Global Financial Crisis reveals several things. The first is the literal and metaphorical wall that the U.S. finance industry erected to keep the Titans securely in control. The second is that Greece's genius loci is complex and, at times, conflicting. No wonder ancient Greece had a polytheistic religion whose gods often argued, and Themis's presence was required. The gods and goddesses also seemed to hold the diversity of Greece's soul. For instance, Aphrodite captures the beauty and waters of the islands, Demeter reflects the divinity of Nature, and Athena holds the wisdom of civilization and progress. For the Greek people, economic development may need to take the many archetypal energies into account, including those who honor the Earth. Lessons from the Lenape people would echo the same thing for the U.S.

The third revelation is that a terrapsychological view of Greece reveals long-standing open cultural wounds, which are critical to keep in mind because many of the experts' criticisms of Greece during the Global Financial Crisis are actually symptoms of unhealed trauma. As the next chapters will show, this is also true of the United States. Thus, Greece's red thread leads us toward the need to tend to cultural traumas for economic health and development.

References

Beaton, R. (2019). *Greece: Biography of a modern nation*. Allen Lane.

Benaki Museum. (2019 June 21–2019 September 22). *The same river twice: Contemporary art in Athens*. Athens.

Casey, E. S. (2009). *Getting back into place: Toward a renewed understanding of the place-world* (2nd ed.). Indiana University Press.

Chalquist, C., & Barnwell, G. (2023). Introduction: Everything converses. In C. Chalquist & G. Barnwell (Eds.), *Terrapsychology: Further inquiry into self, place, and planet* (pp. 1–10). Routledge.

Coppin, J., & Nelson, E. (2005). *The art of inquiry: A depth psychological perspective*. Spring Publications.

Degnan Smith, J. (2023). A terrapsychological engagement of the elusive Eleusis. In C. Chalquist & G. Barnwell (Eds.), *Terrapsychology: Further inquiry into self, place, and planet* (pp. 11–21). Routledge.

Donleavy, P., & Shearer, A. (2008). *From ancient myth to modern healing: Themis: Goddess of heart-soul, justice and reconciliation*. Routledge.

Edinger, E. F. (1994). *The eternal drama: The inner meaning of Greek mythology*. Shambhala Publications, Inc.

Hillman, J. (2006). *City & soul*. R. J. Leaver (Ed.). Spring Publications, Inc.

Kalsched, D. (2013). *Trauma and the soul: A psycho-spiritual approach to human development and its interruption*. Routledge.

Kiehl, J. T. (2016). *Facing climate change: An integrated path to the future*. Columbia University Press.

Kouveli, A., Dollis, N., & Leonard, J. (Eds.). (2017). *Acropolis museum guide* (J. Leonard, Trans.). En Typo-Kalogerogiannis (Original work published 2017).

Llewellyn Smith, M. (2004). *Athens: A cultural and literary history*. Interlink Books.

Milatovic, J., & Sanfey, P. (2015 September 17). 10 things you need to know about the Greek economy. European Bank for Reconstruction and Development. Retrieved from https://www.ebrd.com/news/2015/10-things-you-need-to-know-about-the-greek-economy.html

Ministry of Culture. (2018 December 26–2019 June 30). *Occupied Athens during World War II*. Athens.

Paris, G. (1986). *Pagan meditations: Aphrodite, Hestia, Artemis*. Spring Publications, Inc.

Pritchard, E. T. (2002). *Native New Yorkers: The legacy of the Algonquin people of New York*. Council Oak Books.

Rasche, J. (2016). Introduction. In J. Rasche & T. Singer (Eds.), *Europe's many souls: Exploring cultural complexes and identities* (pp. 15–31). Spring Journal, Inc.

Sabini, M. (2002). *The earth has a soul: C.G. Jung on nature, technology & modern life*. North Atlantic Books.

Slater, G. (2024). *Jung vs. Borg: Finding the deeply human in a posthuman age*. Winter Press.

Tarnas, R. (2013). *Is the modern psyche undergoing a rite of passage?* Retrieved from Cosmos and Psyche: https://cosmosandpsyche.files.wordpress.com/2013/05/revision-rite-of-passage.pdf

Tooze, A. (2018). *Crashed: How a decade of financial crises changed the world*. Penguin.

Tsempelis, E. (2016). The inner riddle of "Greek psychic debt". In J. Rasche & T. Singer (Eds.), *Europe's many souls: Exploring cultural complexes and identities* (pp. 71–92). Spring Journal, Inc.

5 A Wounded View

When viewed through a depth psychological lens, many of the "idiosyncrasies" of Greek culture that economists and sociologists have identified as contributing to the crisis reflect unhealed trauma. We may never know which cultural aspects arise from Greece's experiences, such as war (nurture), or stem from Greece's inherent essence (nature); the debate over nature versus nurture remains unresolved. However, given the impact of open wounds on the well-being of individuals and communities, it makes sense to consider cultural issues through a trauma lens. Perhaps some of Greece's essence, like its natural multiplicity and splinteredness, has been exacerbated and solidified by its wars and hardships. It is also crucial to consider open wounds because trauma and its resulting behaviors cannot be addressed through criticism or logical approaches. Instead, the imagination and unconscious must be engaged to find reconciliation and restoration.

Addressing unhealed cultural wounds is a moral imperative for the well-being of individuals and communities. However, it is also a practical economic concern, as unresolved trauma can result in behaviors that undermine a group's overall health; a group with unresolved issues may engage in self-sabotage. Understanding trauma in relation to economic health is essential because many communities facing the harshest socioeconomic conditions are those that have endured unimaginable violence and harm due to factors such as their religion, nationality, gender, sexuality, and skin color. Almost any population that has experienced war, colonialism, or significant ecological disasters is likely to be burdened by the effects of trauma.

A Traumatized Psyche

Donald Kalsched expanded on the work of Jung, Freud, and other theorists to develop a comprehensive theory describing the impact of trauma on a person's inner world. Thomas Singer recognized the importance of applying the theory to collective trauma. Both scholars noted that reactions to trauma and pain are deeply rooted, archetypal, automatic mechanisms for survival.

DOI: 10.4324/9781003497622-5

According to Kalsched (2013), when a person faces more than they can consciously endure, such as child abuse or the horrors of war, the psyche endures "a life-saving split" called dissociation that distributes the emotional impact to different parts of the psyche and soma (p. 11). This mechanism prevents the person from facing the entirety of the trauma, which could be psychologically fatal. The outcome is a new inner architecture of the psyche, where the various parts "cease to know about each other" (p. 11). A false self is developed to present a facade to the outside world, safeguarding the true, inner, sacred self of the individual. Defenses that are archetypal in nature are established to help cope with difficult events. While these defenses are life-saving, they are also fragmenting, leaving an individual not entirely alive and with "inner deforming mirrors" that distort their self-perception into something "less than, and different from, the real person that we are" (p. 159). Additionally, this creates a division between the ego and the unconscious, as well as the soul, potentially hindering psychological development. It often results in a split between the psyche and soma, causing disembodiment.

The imagination is engaged to create a mythological story to hold the pain of the survivor and the fragmented parts of the psyche until it is bearable to speak about personally (Kalsched, 2013, p. 11). This is a productive use of the imagination and archetypal worlds. Kalsched noted Trousdale's words: "Trauma produces a heightened drama of heroes and victims whose more ordinary human story is waiting to be told" (Trousdell, 2011, p. 131). A drama with heroes and victims is clearly seen in Greece's experience of the crisis.

The architecture of the traumatized psyche includes a "regressed" part of the personality that appears child-like, as well as a "progressed" aspect that can serve as a helpful guardian but can also quickly become sadistic and tyrannical (Kalsched, 2013, p. 12). This leads to a love-hate relationship with the true self. The progressed, persecutory part operates like an autoimmune disease, attacking the healthy aspects of the personality, targeting its divine and animated elements (p. 13). The individual may lose hope, caught in a repetition compulsion where they repeat the same self-defeating behaviors. They possess a fragile ego and fluctuate between feeling inflated and feeling depressed (p. 132). Additionally, they may project this inner aggressor onto others, positioning themselves as a victim to a masochistic counterpart.

One of the most challenging aspects of suffering trauma is the loss of the capacity to be creative due to a disconnection from the unconscious and the symbolic world. Instead, the individual shifts to fantasy, which is not a productive imaginal space but rather one of a "melancholic self-soothing compromise which goes on forever" (Kalsched, 1996, p. 35). This often results in a person rewriting their own history, omitting painful memories, and not processing and transforming the trauma. Healing can be difficult. It requires a journey into the shadows to recognize the defenses and false self, which may evoke strong emotions and a sense of crucifixion and death because it often necessitates a sacrifice of the ego and a sense of identity to recover the lost parts of the Self (Kalsched, 2013, p. 128).

Singer (2004) argued that these symptoms of trauma also show up in collective culture. A traumatized group will mobilize defenses to protect the collective spirit and the group ego from a sense of destruction. The group may also present a false self to the world to protect its vulnerable and authentic aspects. Its persecutory aspect may also "develop a cohort of protector/persecutor leaders" who may protect or violently torture the people (p. 19). It may also find itself in a repetition compulsion.

Groups also engage with the mythopoetic imagination to craft a narrative or myth that shapes their self-perception and their role in the world. This can be observed in the cultural events and symbols found in their communities.

> The countless rituals of commemoration, ceremonies, and national anniversaries, celebrating everything from the founding of the country, to victories of war, to the naming of streets and libraries after heroes, are attempts to establish living monuments to a history that represents the group. These modes of remembering create a connective tissue that binds the group and individuals in an interconnected worldview composed of shared history, values, rules, outlook, and a sense of group spirit.
>
> (Kimbles, 2006, pp. 100–101)

Thus, listening to cultural stories is critical to understanding a group, and by hearing them through a metaphorical ear, the gods and goddesses reveal the archetypes and defenses at play.

Images of a Wounded Greece

One day, I was riding a tram in Athens when it suddenly came to a stop. An announcement was made, and everyone got off. Since I spoke very little Greek, I remained there, hoping it would start again, but it didn't. Later, I read in the news that the cement under parts of the track was crumbling, revealing the river Ilissos beneath. In ancient times, the sacred river was home to the nine muses and various temples dedicated to the gods. It was also where preparations for the Eleusinian mysteries took place. The covering and disconnection from the sacred waters may symbolize the Greeks' disconnection from the sacred Self and the soul. However, due to the crumbling concrete, the government considered uncovering the rivers, restoring the banks, and creating parks. This seemed like a powerful metaphor for removing the defenses that arise from trauma and reconnecting with the soul. As Chalquist (2007) noted:

> Cover a place's history and vitality in asphalt, concrete, or forgetfulness, and it returns an episode at a time in symptoms, in dreams, in folklore,

> crime, public politics, or private fights until brought fully into the present through conscious reflection.
>
> (p. 7)

This seemed true for Greece; it was as though it sought to bring these open wounds to the surface to tend to them.

One of the first indications of trauma may be the GFC experts' observations that Greece stumbles from disaster to disaster, which may point to a repetition compulsion stemming from unhealed trauma. Many experts have also noted that Greece suffers from a lack of identity and sense of self. Tsempelis (2016) argued that Greece was experiencing a sense of false consciousness and that this moment presented an opportunity to discover its true destiny. Beaton (2019) also identified a Greek identity crisis, asserting that they "have found themselves forced to take stock, to look again at their history, at the values they grew up with, at their own sense of who they are and where they belong in the world" (p. 394). Nikos Dimou, a controversial figure criticized for his views on the Greek people, claims that he shares his reflections from a place of deep love for them. Dimou (2013) pointed out the "lost face" of the Greeks, arguing that "we are a people without a face. Without identity. Not because we don't have a face. But because we don't dare look at ourselves in the mirror" (p. 15). This also reflects the feelings of shame that can emerge in trauma victims.

Many experts have noted the oscillation of the Greek people between feeling like a divine child and experiencing a profound sense of shame, which reflects the new self-care system emerging from trauma. Verouchi (2015) emphasized the Greek identification with the divine child persecuted by those envious of them. Additionally, Kalyvas (2015) observed that Greeks tend to exhibit "self-aggrandizement" and "a sense of insecurity and a feeling of persecution," consistently feeling the need to be defensive (p. 5). The divine child burdened with shame is encapsulated in the Greek saying about themselves: "We gave the world light and held onto the darkness" (Angelos, 2016, p. 12).

The mythological figure of Hephaestus embodies a sense of shame and feeling "less than." He was the only wounded Olympian god, and his mother, Hera, rejected him for this reason. His temple in the Agora, the heart of ancient Athens, is the most well-preserved in modern times, perhaps reflecting that the part of the Greeks who were somehow wounded, rejected, and born wrong may still be intact.

This conflicting sense of self-worth is also captured in the street art image by Dimitris Taxis of a child who is held up with elements of its glorious past, such as democracy and Socrates, yet weighed down with more challenging aspects, such as their economics and Athens' focus on luxury. Dimou argued that many Greeks feel entitled to join the EU simply because of their nation's grandeur. He (2013) also described Greece's two national inferiority complexes: "the one in time—with the ancient Greeks. The other in space—with the 'Europeans'" (p. 13). Interestingly, stories of the divine child, including Jesus Christ and the Greek God Zeus, are two ruling god images that have played a significant role in Greek culture and religion, which will be discussed in Chapter 7.

Dimou (2013) also indicated that this sense of shame is reflected in how the place of Greece is treated: "Somewhere inside us we believe that we don't deserve to live in such a lovely land. And we try to bring it into line with our own standards. Our own level. So we cover it with concrete and refuse" (p. 32). This may explain Athens' cement blanket.

Greece's gaps and dislocation from history are reflected in the place of Athens. Llewelyn Smith (2004) highlighted Greece's disjointed architectural history in his description of an exhibition about Athens in 2002. The Greek architects' display noted that Athens avoided the usual European traditions in its town planning and architecture and instead "imposed its own rhythms, shapes and concepts, which are characterized by nasty words like caesura and separation, disruption, inversion, instantaneity and excess, voids, gaps, incompleteness, and disproportion" (p. 208). The caesurea is experienced in the separation of the commercial city from the archaeological sites which indicates that, unlike other ancient cities such as Rome, "the historical layers of Athens are not integrated into the modern city, but are cut off from it" (p. 208).

Greece also shows some signs of Singer's (2004) observation that victims of trauma may unconsciously create a leadership of oppressors. Beaton (2019) described that in modern history, Greece has seldom ruled itself and frequently required financial help from its rulers. This point may be seen in the elected Greek government, whose misspending of funds left the country in great debt. It may also be seen in the Troika, who were forced into a position of making difficult demands of the Greek people, although they took it too far.

There are also indications of a Greek resistance to reality, which many scholars pointed out. The avoidance of responsibility is seen in the Greek game of *ballaki euthinon* or "little ball of blame" which gets kicked around (Palaiologos, 2015, p. x). Tsempelis (2016) noted that most of the Greek people still either deny the crisis or consider it someone else's fault: "the Germans, the capitalists, the politicians—the list is long" (p. 82). This inability to face and metabolize the shadow may also be seen metaphorically in Greece's fraught relationship with garbage, those things that we would like to discard. Garbage collection and disposal have historically been problematic in Greece. Palaiologos (2015) referred to a European Commission report published in 2012 that found that Greece was at the very bottom of the rankings for its waste management policies, with only one of its 71 landfills compliant with EU regulations.

The Greek people seem to have engaged mythopoetic imagery to endure the traumas, particularly the suffering hero fighting insurmountable odds. They portray themselves as victims of the corruption of capitalism and the greed and domination of more powerful forces. Dimou's (2013) commented that as Greeks, "we're saved by our mythopoeia. As soon as (for whatever reason) the tyrants fall or the foreigners leave- we leap up (like Karaghiozis with the Dragon) and say: 'It was we who got rid of them!'" (p. 19). Beaton (2019) noted the role of the hero during the War of Independence and in the Polytechnic uprising as the "heroes of the Polytechnic" became "seared into public memory" (p. 338). He also identified the importance of freedom in their heroic fights: "Freedom meant absolute self-sufficiency, the refusal to acknowledge any authority other than their own" (p. 88).

Dimou (2013) noted the Greeks' deep identification with the hero: "Whenever a Greek looks at himself in the mirror, he sees either Alexander the Great or Kolokotronis (hero of the Greek War of Independence) or (at least) Onassis. Never Karaghiozis" who is a popular comic puppet character in Greek shadow theater (p. 4). During the crisis, a quote attributed to Churchill floated around on Greek social media, commending the Greeks' resistance to the Italians and Germans in the Second World War: "We will not say hereafter that the Greeks fight like heroes, but heroes fight like Greeks."

The image of the hero is seen in a speech written by Varoufakis for the prime minister, Alexis Tsipras, when he was forced to concede to the Troika's demands:

> Fellow Greeks. We have fought valiantly against an ironclad troika of creditors. We gave it our all. Alas, it is hard to argue with creditors who do not want their money back. We faced down the world's strongest institutions, the local oligarchy, powers much greater than ours. We have received no help from anyone… We are not giving up. Today I am signaling to you to fight another day. Tomorrow morning I shall accede to the troika's demands. But only because this war has many battles ahead.
>
> (Varoufakis, 2017, p. 433)

Perhaps more disturbing than the victim and brave, suffering hero is Beaton's (2019) argument that Greece's metaphor for itself is the canary sent into the coal mine to detect poisonous gasses. Greece sees itself as the "small, weak songbird whose life could be sacrificed for the greater good" (p. 397). Thus, victimhood becomes martyrdom, and Greece becomes a scapegoat.

The Greek people have a long-standing relationship with the hero, including the hero cults of ancient Greece. Thus, it could be argued that the hero is a part of Greece's genius loci. It is also true that Greece's history has required the people to engage with the hero to protect the inner soul. However, the hero who saved Greece many times over millennia may not save their economic situation. As Jung (1943/1966) said, "If heroism becomes chronic, it ends in a cramp, and the cramp leads to catastrophe or to neurosis or both" (para. 41). Shalit (2008) also noted the problems that occur when the hero is simply about the ego "a hero without a shadow is like an ego without a soul," and when this happens, there is a sense of emptiness or meaninglessness (p. 26).

The mythic figure who holds images of hero, victim, and scapegoat is that of Dionysus. Despite his connections to wine and hedonism, Dionysus is quite a complex character. He is associated with revolutions and a drive for freedom, as well as emotions, including hysteria and depression. There is a deep connection between Dionysus, the god of theater and tragedy, and heroes "for he was the hero among the gods," and his cult was "full of the sufferings of the heroes" (Kerenyi, 1959, p. 14). Dionysus was the liberator and revolutionary.

Alexander the Great emulated Dionysus, even minting coins with his own image, wearing a headdress adorned with Dionysus's elephant. Alexander is still one of the greatest heroes of modern Greek people, and retaining the right to his heritage and his name was a part of the major conflict with the neighboring Republic of Northern Macedonia. The disputes caused bigger protests than the financial crisis itself.

Dionysus was also known as the divine child and was seen as the god who opposed the Titans, who tore him to pieces and ate all of him except for his heart, which Athena saved. Dionysus was then reborn by Zeus and Semele. His myth of death and resurrection is often equated to that of the crucified Christ, which is prevalent in modern Greek culture. Easter is one of the most important holidays in the Greek Orthodox Church, which will be discussed further in Chapter 7.

The Greek people may have identified with the ideal of Dionysus, seeing themselves resisting and being torn apart by Titanic powers. This idealization prevents them from embracing the more shadowy and difficult aspects of the Dionysian archetype, which include violence. They also have lost touch with Dionysus's potential for deep transformation, which will be discussed further in the next chapter.

Images of a Wounded U.S.A.

Greece does not have a monopoly on the hero, the divine child, or the quest for freedom. These are all alive and well in the United States, as are gaping cultural wounds. Despite some movements to heal and make amends for such things as slavery and the treatment of Native peoples, there is still unhealed trauma.

Given the violence they instigated, it is hard to view the early colonialists as victims of trauma. However, Carta (2020) pointed out that the early settlers were fleeing religious persecution while seeking economic and religious freedom. Leaving the old world represented a loss, a trauma that resulted in defenses (p. 19). They also faced numerous hardships, enduring harsh weather conditions.

The early colonialists adopted images of the Puritans, who had "heavenly origin" and were tasked with fulfilling God's grace through a manifest destiny (Carta, 2020, p. 14). This idea of being the chosen ones, like Greece's experience, leads to a denial of the shadow; "The Puritan is sheltered in the safety of his predestined goodness" (p. 17). The image of the Puritan, combined with images of the pioneer discovering new lands, led the early people to see themselves as pioneers for God. This has allowed the U.S. to have carte blanche to do what it wants because it is on a divine mission:

> The United States is the predestined country whose purpose is to realize the Kingdom of God on Earth (unfortunately, since the 19th century this purpose has been transformed into the urge to commodify the Earth, which is rapidly leading to its destruction).
>
> (p. 17)

The combination of the Puritan and pioneer has forged a capitalist system that consumes and exploits without conscience or hesitation. It also leads the U.S. to see itself as the heroic force conquering evil. The new land of the U.S. was viewed as safe, while everything outside was regarded as hostile and evil (Carta, 2020, p. 15). A brief review of U.S. history in places like Vietnam or Panama serves as a reminder of the U.S.'s capacity for evil.

West (2020) argued that the challenging foundations of the U.S. created an Alpha Narcissistic America with a "ruthless determination to dominate" and finds that;

> Huge amounts of our national wealth, both economic and environmental, are in the unregulated hands of people for whom amassing and spending more and more of it is a thrill, a challenge, and yet another star on their shield. Insatiable greed partners with the drive to win every time.
>
> (p. 231)

Images of Alpha Narcissists appear on the big screen in *The Big Short* and the Lenape's two-colored snake.

The greed, arrogance, and power drive seen in the U.S. may partially result from the wounds at the foundations of colonialism. From a Jungian perspective, it is also critical to consider the instinctual elements of human life and the existence of the Titanic elements in the psyche, which are difficult to contain but must be addressed. Along with a focus on healing cultural and personal wounds, these also need to be considered in dysfunctional and harmful behaviors.

The Call for the Depth Psychological Hero

The hero myth has been used in depth psychology as a metaphor for psychological development. The heroic part of the ego ventures into the shadow, overcoming elements of complexes and trauma, resulting in a change in perspective (Shalit, 2008). The hero's journey is to fight his own defenses, "the demons of his own creation," by courageously engaging with reality and "transcending the illusions of felt curses, handicaps, bogeymen, and 'monsters'" (Kalsched, 2013, pp. 211–212). Through this process, one can distinguish between genuine fears and defenses, which allows a re-engagement with life. The process also helps a group to reclaim the disowned parts of themselves that have been projected onto others, which is the area of inquiry in the next chapter.

The hero must go into the dark of the unconscious to redeem the soul or a forgotten myth and bring it back to the light, to consciousness. Crises often provide opportunities to do the work of the depth psychological hero. Tsempelis (2016) recognized Greece's economic crisis as an opportunity for Greece to find its true destiny.

The hero brings something new to consciousness as "the hero revolts against an ego that has stiffened in the grips of habits and conventions, an ego that has become empty behind the emperor's new clothes, whether within the personal psyche or that of society" (Shalit, 2008, pp. 137–138). Thus, parts of the ego must be sacrificed, which is difficult because it requires letting go of our stories about ourselves. People must be willing to see themselves in a new light.

The depth psychological hero must also betray the past to be open to the future. This seems relevant for the financial crisis as both the U.S. and Greece need to betray and release their images of themselves as Puritans, heroes, and divine children to find a way forward. Shalit (2008) quoted Ernst Barlach: "The hero has to 'awaken the sleeping images of the future which can and must come forth from the night, in order to give the world a new and better face'" (p. 137).

Both Greece and the U.S. and global economic health would do well to eschew the egoized, literalized hero and adopt the depth psychological hero. In many great Greek dramas, a hero must overcome seemingly insurmountable challenges, including facing terrible, ferocious enemies. However, the hero must also endure an inner battle with aspects of himself that are as challenging to face as the outer enemy, if not more so. Ultimately, this inner battle also serves the hero in the end. They are stronger and more enlightened. This brings us back to one of Jung's (1954/1967) most well-known quotes; "one does not become enlightened by imagining figures of light, but by making the darkness conscious. The latter procedure, however, is disagreeable, and therefore not popular" (para. 335).

References

Angelos, J. (2016). *The full catastrophe: Travels among the new Greek ruins.* Broadway Books.

Beaton, R. (2019). *Greece: Biography of a modern nation.* Allen Lane.

Carta, S. (2020). Here's Johnny! American carnival in modern times. In T. Singer (Ed.), *Cultural complexes and the soul of America* (pp. 13–34). Routledge.

Chalquist, C. (2007). *Terrapsychology: Reengaging the soul of place*. Spring Journal Books.

Dimou, N. (2013). *On the unhappiness of being Greek*. Zero Books.

Jung, C. G. (1966). On the psychology of the unconscious (R. F. C. Hull, Trans.). In H. Read et al. (Eds.), *The collected works of C. G. Jung* (Vol. 7, 2nd ed., pp. 1–119). Princeton University Press (Original work published 1943).

Jung, C. G. (1967). The philosophical tree (R. F. C. Hull, Trans.). In H. Read et al. (Eds.), *The collected works of C. G. Jung* (Vol. 13, pp. 251–349). Princeton University Press (Original work published 1954).

Kalsched, D. (1996). *The inner world of trauma: Archetypal defenses of the personal spirit*. Routledge.

Kalsched, D. (2013) *Trauma and the soul: A psycho-spiritual approach to human development and its interruption*. Routledge.

Kalyvas, S. N. (2015). *Modern Greece: What everyone needs to know*. Oxford University Press.

Kerenyi, C. (1959). *The heroes of the Greeks*. Thames and Hudson.

Kimbles, S. L. (2006). Cultural complexes and the transmission of group traumas in everyday life. *Psychological Perspectives*, *49*(1), 96–110.

Llewellyn Smith, M. (2004). *Athens: A cultural and literary history*. Interlink Books.

Palaiologos, Y. (2015). *The 13th labour of Hercules: Inside the Greek crisis*. Portobello Books.

Shalit, E. (2008). *Enemy, cripple & beggar: Shadows in the hero's path*. Fisher King Press.

Singer, T. (2004). The cultural complex and archetypal defenses of the group spirit: Baby Zeus, Elian Gonzales, "Constantine's sword, and other holy ways (with special attention to 'axis of evil'). In T. Singer & S. L. Kimbles (Eds.), *The cultural complex: Contemporary Jungian perspectives on psyche and society* (pp. 13–33). Routledge.

Trousdell, R. (2011). Surviving trauma, becoming human: Victim and hero roles in the Oresteia of Aeschylus. In V. Beane Rutter & T. Singer (Eds.), *Ancient Greece, modern psyche: Archetypes in the making* (pp. 131–158). Spring Journal Books.

Tsempelis, E. (2016). The inner riddle of "Greek psychic debt". In J. Rasche & T. Singer (Eds.), *Europe's many souls; Exploring cultural complexes and identities* (pp. 71–92). Spring Journal, Inc.

Varoufakis, Y. (2017). *Adults in the room: My battle with the European and American deep establishment*. Farrar, Straus and Giroux.

Verouchi, V. (2015). *Cultural barriers to prosperity: The case of Greece* [Working Paper]. Retrieved from The Fletcher School Tufts University: https://sites.tufts.edu/karamanlischair/files/2018/12/Karamanlis-Working-Papers-2015-No-3.pdf

West, J. (2020). Our divisible nation: In the grip of an alpha narcissistic complex. In T. Singer (Ed.), *Cultural complexes and the soul of America* (pp. 221–238). Routledge.

6 A Complex View

The presence of unhealed trauma leads directly to Jung's concept of the complex, which he regarded as the royal road to the unconscious, albeit more like a "rough and uncommonly devious footpath" (Jung, 1948/1969b, para. 210). As discussed in Chapter 1, the complex was one of Jung's most profound psychological insights. The unconscious, autonomous, splinter personalities significantly impact people's lives. Everyone has complexes, which are not always problematic. However, when activated, they can lead to

> a situation in which one's entire personality is being held hostage by a cluster of emotions associated with a particular set of archetypal images and experiences; a clouding of consciousness occurs and one, alas, is no longer the master of one's house.
>
> (Tsempelis, 2019, pp. 191–192)

Thomas Singer and Samuel Kimbles recognized that groups of people can also have complexes and developed the concept of the cultural complex by integrating Jung's theory of complexes with Henderson's (1990) idea of the cultural unconscious, which refers to "an area of historical memory that lies between the collective unconscious and the manifest pattern of the culture" (p. 103).

The power of culture cannot be underestimated, as business consultant Peter Drucker aptly expressed in his statement, "Culture eats strategy for breakfast." People's unconscious beliefs, norms, and behaviors can undermine their goals and ambitions. Edward Hall's Iceberg Model of Culture is a fitting image for this idea. Like an iceberg, only a tiny portion of culture is visible. Most elements of culture, much like the iceberg, remain out of view—submerged in the water or the unconscious. The unseen and unknown aspects of culture, akin to the submerged ice, can potentially sink even the mightiest of ships, including a nation's economic health. By examining culture and economics through a cultural complex lens, we can discern at least the silhouette of the perilous underwater glacier.

DOI: 10.4324/9781003497622-6

Cultural complexes help explain why groups of people act the way they do, including their everyday behavior related to their economic lives. This sheds light on why individuals do not always act in their best interest or out of concern for the planet. Cultural complexes also reveal unhealed cultural wounds, as they show "what happens to the psyche of a people when unconscious forces stimulated by social, economic, religious, and other disruptive forces reawaken old conflicts and wounds that then give way to the breakthrough of destructive archetypal influences" (Singer, 2016, p. 5). The Global Financial Crisis created an ideal environment for cultural complexes to surface.

Working with Cultural Complexes

Many metaphors emerge when discussing cultural complexes, including a teratoma that "has bits and pieces of thought, memory, affect, and behavior that glom together in a mass that defies rationality but very powerfully influences, even takes over, the more everyday 'tissue' of social reality that surrounds it" (Singer, 2014, p. 7). Cultural complexes are passed down through the generations and encompass numerous aspects of human experiences, including history, religion, economics, and anthropology. They shape the identities and actions of the members, forming a "living reality of ideas, beliefs, memories, feelings, images, and behavior in the psyche" (Singer, 2016, p. 6). Cultural complexes give a group a sense of self and their place in the world.

Cultural complexes, which can range from fairly normal to quite pathological, possess several characteristics (Singer, 2020). They can be either dormant or active. Similar to personal complexes, they are autonomous, suggesting they seem to have a life of their own and are not controlled by the rational mind. Cultural complexes are repetitive, continually expressing the same "emotional and ideological content" (p. xxii). They are rigid; they resist facts and change and "collect experiences and memories that validate their own point of view" (p. xxii). Cultural complexes are usually simplistic and black and white and are accompanied by strong emotions. Finally, cultural complexes are frequently connected to a nation's founding narrative, including its ancestors and beliefs about its mission.

Cultural complexes can be observed by paying attention to the feelings, images, memories, behaviors, and stereotypical thoughts that recur with a complex (Singer, 2016;2020). To really understand cultural complexes, they need to be explored and considered from different perspectives (Rasche, 2016, p. 23). This provides an opportunity to reveal and work with the emotions at the center of the complex, which is critical to lessening their impact. Unfortunately, most academic disciplines disregard emotions despite the prominent role they play in people's lives (Rasche, 2016).

As discussed in the previous chapter, one of the challenges of working with cultural complexes is that they require groups to face the collective shadow and consider their culpability in their difficult situation. This seems particularly unfair to ask of people who have endured trauma, yet it is critical to curtailing problematic behaviors and ultimately bringing psychological relief. Jung (1951/1969c) argued that becoming conscious of shadow material is a "moral problem" that requires "recognizing the dark aspects of the personality as present and real" (para. 14). It is also the path toward healing and growth because working with cultural complexes "can serve as a stimulus for society's individuation, if it is up to the task to bring consciousness to its collective psychological and social conflicts rather than continuously acting them out" (Singer, 2011, p. xiv).

Complexes must be looked at symbolically to reveal the archetypes that lie underneath. By looking at the complex through a mythological lens, we can see the gods in the wounds. The complex must be "laid at the proper altar because it makes a difference to our suffering and perhaps to the God who is there manifesting" (Hillman, 1976, p. 104). So, we go in search of the gods and goddesses in economics again, beginning with those in the United States.

The U.S.'s Complexes in Economics and the GFC

Singer (2020) argued for the necessity of examining cultural complexes in the U.S. because "when American cultural complexes contribute to the destruction of the country and the rest of the world, it does matter that they exist" (p. xxiv). The U.S. has many complexes, a couple of which are particularly relevant to the dysfunctions of the economic system, including the U.S.'s obsession with achievement and wealth and the prioritization of personal freedom over the needs of the collective:

> One of the highest values in American society has been the accumulation of personal wealth and material goods, often at the expense of or in disregard for the common good. This complex emphasizes individual achievement in the material world…The negative side of this emphasizes the collective and individual right to eat the world, own the world, amass personal wealth, and continuously increase the "gross national product." In the name of participating in the American Dream, consumerism in the United States has become equated with the highest good.
>
> (p. xxvii)

As discussed in the Chapter 5, these complexes appear to have formed from the wounds inflicted during the colonization of the U.S., becoming part of the founding myth. They are deeply rooted in the "American Dream" and the land of opportunity. However, they significantly contributed to the Global Financial Crisis. The insatiable drive to grow, possess, and consume reflects our old friends, the Titans, and their ambition and desire to dominate.

The U.S. is also ensnared in a freedom complex that arose from its struggle for independence from Britain. Freedom is deeply ingrained in the Constitution and the founding ideals reflected in the Declaration of Independence's assertion of "life, liberty, and the pursuit of happiness." While the emphasis on freedom is understandable for those who have been oppressed, it can transform into a different form of oppression when it ignores the truth that no one is genuinely free from responsibility and limitations, nor from their impact on others and the Earth. The U.S. has lost the systemic awareness that we are all interconnected, part of a larger whole to which everyone bears responsibility. The Global Financial Crisis, along with the COVID-19 pandemic, has shown that national borders cannot contain microorganisms or crises.

This drive for freedom is coupled with a need for newness. Hillman (n.d.) argued that "newness still remains America's prison" (para. 34). It "governs our endeavors; developing land, developing economics, products, technologies, our personality. We value even the arts in terms of new developments" (para. 33). The New Land, the pioneering spirit, and the frontier mentality leave little space for the elders and their profound wisdom, which erodes heritage, environment, and community. The puer, in the form of Icarus, rushes away from the earth, flying too close to the sun.

As noted in the last chapter, the U.S. is vying with Greece for the position of divine child. Seeing itself as the "new land" reflects a sense of superiority in the U.S. (Singer, 2020, p. xxviii), as does seeing itself as "having a special relationship to God" (p. xxvii). These ideas around religion and cultural complexes will be explored extensively in the next chapter. However, one thing to reiterate here is that if a nation perceives itself as the chosen one, it makes shadow work difficult because there is no rationale for doing so: since we are the divine child, we can do no wrong.

Thus, a mythic view again invokes images of the Titanic and the puer, who seem to be wreaking havoc in the global economy. The dynamic between them is seen between Greece and Germany and within Greece and Germany themselves.

Transforming Cultural Complexes

Cultural complexes have two sides. An inner one that structures the collective psyche of the group and an outer one that creates the face that the group shows the world. This outer face only exists in relation to another group: "There is no nation without its neighbor" (Rasche, 2016, p. 26). This interrelatedness means that "if a cultural or national complex is to be transformed this may only be possible in relation to the transformation of the neighbor's complex" (p. 26). Thus, we need to look at cultural complexes in relation to each other.

One nation's criticisms of its neighbor often reflect aspects of its own shadow, although there is typically an element of truth; the neighbor provides a "hook" for projection. Jung (1916/1969a) noted this dynamic of denial and projection during WWI:

> As events in wartime have clearly shown, our mentality is distinguished by the shameless naivete with which we judge our enemy, and in the judgment we pronounce upon him we unwittingly reveal our own defects: we simply accuse our enemy of our own unadmitted faults.
>
> (para. 516)

When a cultural complex is activated, the group will project a particular image onto themselves and then project another image onto the "other" group (Perry, 1970). These images are not entirely based on reality and are usually dripping with emotion. For instance, the U.S. often projects the image of a hero and fighter for freedom and democracy onto themselves and often projects an image of a tyrant or cruel bully onto other nations. However, the U.S. certainly has its tyrannical and bullying moments. Transforming the complex requires the nation to own those eschewed elements; for example, the U.S. needs to acknowledge its shadow side, which requires a change in identity to include these darker elements.

The dynamic of one nation projecting its shadow material onto another nation is clearly seen in the relationship between Greece and Germany during the financial crisis. Their cultural complexes mirror and reinforce each other. Viewing their relationship through a mythic and cultural complex lens shows the archetypes at play between and within Greece and Germany and in economics more widely.

A Complex View of Complexes: Greece and Germany

The Greek people maintain a love-hate relationship with Germany, admiring its discipline and high-quality products while also scorning its seriousness and work ethic (Dimou, 2015). The German people, in turn, greatly admire ancient Greece (Dimou, 2015; Beaton, 2019). Germany has played a crucial role in excavating Greece's ancient treasures and reviving the works of ancient Greek writers.

During the crisis, the general perception was one in which "the image of the heartless, cold and disciplinarian Germans hovers over Greece—while in Germany the talk is of the lazy, greedy and spendthrift Greeks who milk the German taxpayer" (Dimou, 2015, para. 1). These ideas were conveyed in various ways, such as through political cartoons, comedians, news reports, and media. They were also illustrated in the street art of two ancient Greek people in togas holding signs. One sign states, "This is all because of EU," which picks up on Greece's tendency to blame the EU and Germany for its problems during the crisis, while the other sign reads, "You're so drachmatic" which plays on the ancient Greek coin, the drachma, and the perception that the Greek people are overly emotional and exaggerate. The dynamic between the two countries was also seen in the words and arguments of the Greek and German finance ministers during the crisis: Yanis Varoufakis and the late Wolfgang Schäuble (Beaton, 2019).

A Mythic View of Greece's Complex

Many Greek communications during the crisis described the Greek people as heroes struggling against austerity, the corruption of capitalism, and the domination of Europe, particularly Germany, to which various Nazi references were made. Beaton (2019) noted the cry of the political left during the elections taking place in the depths of the crisis that "little Greece would stand up to the bullying creditors in the European Union and the IMF" (p. 385). As discussed in Chapter 3, the Greek people saw themselves, in some ways accurately, as the scapegoat for the EU. The need to protest and revolt, including against the perceived misdeeds of their own government, was seen in Loukanikos, one of the stray dogs in Athens, who barked on the front lines of the protests. He became an international legend and *Time* magazine's Personalities of the Year nominee in 2011.

When viewed through a mythological lens, we discover images of the hero Dionysus. Dionysus is connected to Greece's foundational myth. His death at the hands of the Titans and his subsequent rebirth through violence and bloodshed mirrors modern Greece's resurgence after the Revolution. Given the Titans' destruction of Dionysus, it is understandable that the Greek people projected the image of the Titans onto the German government, portraying it as cold, greedy, corrupt, oppressive, and unappreciative of Greece's uniqueness. Street art in Athens depicted a pig holding money, with the commentary, "Hands of gold are always cold."

Greece also projected the thief Hermes onto Germany, accusing it of being more interested in extracting money from Greece to save its own banks than in helping Greece to recover. This accusation was not unfounded. Hermes is slippery and has a knack for escaping tricky situations; he "was the god of holes—loop, key, and ass—always capable of finding the right threshold through which to make a way" (Schenk, 2012, p. 153).

As anticipated, many of Greece's accusations against Germany were elements of the Greek shadow, including the presence of Hermes, whose mercurial nature was there from the beginning when the Greek government fudged their numbers to qualify to join the Euro. He was also present in government corruption and tax evasion, which are, of course, not unique to Greece. Too much Hermes leaves little room for his counterpart Apollo, who, despite quite a bit of bad press, helps plan and achieve goals—skills the Greek government needed to improve.

The curmudgeonly king of the Titans, Saturn, is also prominent in the Greek shadow. The rigidity and hierarchy of Greek banks and the government's excessive regulations suffocate entrepreneurial activity (Palaiologos, 2015, p. 222). Saturn is at the core of Greece's rating of "mostly unfree" in the Index of Economic Freedom.

The Greek people's identification with Dionysus is problematic because he is more complex than his connections to wine, theatre, and heroes. Dionysus is the perpetrator in one of the most violent plays of ancient Greece, Euripides' *Bacchae*. He seeks vengeance against those who deny his divinity, maddening his doubters and causing them to destroy their own children. In idealizing him, the Greek people lose touch with his dark and violent side, and it runs amok in the shadows. As Lopez-Pedraza (2000) pointed out, "identification is the essence of Titanism" (p. 54). Thus, ironically, Greece's identification with Dionysus brings in the Titans.

Lopez-Pedraza (2000) argued that Dionysus is the most repressed god in Western culture because he represents the instinctual, irrational, emotional, bodily, and feminine. He brings in the unconscious, imaginal, and relational and contains the instincts. Dionysus is the "other" who is "a deviance, a mistake, perhaps a monstrosity," and many of his traits have been relegated to the devil by the Christian Church (Paris, 1990, p. 28). He is the god of madness. The ancient Greeks appreciated the need for the Dionysian in civilization, and his presence was seen in the theatres in cities. Dionysus needs to be both honored and contained. However, today's civilization, including economics, holds no place for Dionysus, which leaves him wreaking havoc and seeking his revenge. When Dionysus overcomes the oppressor, he risks becoming the new oppressor with a friendlier face (Paris, 1990). This is often true in revolutions; the new regime ends up being as dominating as the old, if not more so. Greece's anarchist movement has been accused of being tyrannical.

Another aspect of Dionysus that remains in the shadows is his potential for deep relationships, which is critical for the economic health of any community. Dionysus is also capable of profound transformation. The Titans dismembered and devoured Dionysus, except for his heart, which Athena saved. Zeus then consumed Dionysus's heart, and he was reborn with Semele, a mortal, as his mother. His story of death and rebirth reflects the necessity for a conscious sacrifice of the ego and a willingness to confront the shadow to develop a more enlightened perspective. For Greece, this would mean letting go of the jolly Dionysus and the literal hero, moving into the shadows to save the Greek heart, its true self. This would halt the continual unconscious sacrifice that arises from the repetition compulsion, which embodies a Titanic suffering that is "empty, existential, repetitive, and without any possibility of reflection and consciousness" (Lopez-Pedraza, 2000, p. 64).

Engaging with true Dionysian consciousness provides an opportunity to develop the imagination around a group's or individual's story and to rewrite it in a way that helps them to get unstuck from outdated ways of being (Paris,

1990). Dionysian transformation supports the de-literalization of the hero and a re-imagining of identity. Beaton (2019) argued that Greece should see itself as a pioneer, given the hardships it has faced. This could be a more productive image than the one of a suffering hero, however as noted in relation to cultural complexes in the U.S., the pioneer can be problematic if it is given freedom to exploit.

A Mythic View of the German Complex

In Germany, the Aesop fable of the ant and the grasshopper was often used during the crisis (Snow, 2012). Germany represents the ant, working hard all summer to save food for winter. In contrast, Greece is the grasshopper, spending the summer singing and playing; when winter arrives, he must beg the ant for food. Schäuble (Seiradaki, 2012) acknowledged that he could understand Greece's frustration with Germany and its insistence on austerity, but he asserted that it was Greece's responsibility for being reckless and that only by holding Greece accountable for its debts would the necessary reforms occur. This indeed contained some truth.

The Germans projected onto themselves an image of the natural leaders of the Greek gods and goddesses, particularly, Zeus, Apollo, Athena, and the positive side of Saturn, the wise senex, who reflect discipline, intelligence, and a rational perspective. The goddess of war and wisdom, Athena, was born from Zeus's head and remains very bound to her father and his drive for objectivity, judgment, and "the good of the whole" (Hillman, 2007, p. 70). Athena and Zeus keep things rational and practical, just as the Germans aspired to do in the crisis.

Hillman (2007) argued that Athena was the goddess of Western civilization's myth of progress, and she is often contrasted to anyone who brings in excess or the irrational, such as Dionysus; "the dynamic emotionalities, rages, possessions, moist hysterics, depressions, and wild nature outside the *polis* do not belong within the cosmos of Athene's normalization" (p. 69). Like Apollo, Athena moves away from the mythic and into the rational as "we conceive ourselves as social, economic, natural, or political beings rather than as imaginative beings" (p. 72).

Germany projected images of the deceitful Hermes and the indulgent Dionysus onto the Greek populace. The German press labeled the Greek people as bankrupt crooks (Beaton, 2019). Nevertheless, many Germans also empathized with Greece's difficult situation. Like Greece, several of Germany's accusations revealed projected aspects of its own shadow. Hermes undoubtedly lurks in Germany's darkness, alongside the negative traits associated with Saturn. Germany faced criticism for failing to recognize how its dishonest exporting practices contributed to the crisis. The country profited over 2.5 billion euros from interest payments to Greece, prompting calls for Germany to offer Greece some debt relief (Germany Made Billions, 2018). Additionally, the Greek people are not lazy; they work longer hours than anywhere else in Europe (Smith, 2018).

Germany appears to be identified with the civilization of Athena, Apollo, and the wise Senex. Sauer (2016) argued that the Germans have a complex of superiority and feel the need to civilize other nationalities and bring them to "order and rule" (p. 220). These projections do not mean that there is not some truth to the situation. The German government may have felt anxiety and the need to bring control to a chaotic situation where the other parties seemed unwilling or unable to take responsibility.

Sauer (2016) also argued that this sense of superiority may be linked to a long-standing defense mechanism based on a sense of inferiority. To compensate, a need for a critical mission is created, "a sense of knowing the truth and being on a mission" (p. 216). Thus, again, we see the problems of unhealed wounds. Like the U.S. and Greece, Germany is a strong Christian nation and feels "specially blessed by God himself" (p. 222), which makes it prone to projecting anything that challenges its feelings of pureness, including the Dionysian. The English scholar Butler (1935) attributed the Germans' desire to re-engage with ancient Greece and the polytheistic gods to the loss of mysticism in Luther's Christianity.

Like Greece, Germany has its own shadow work and healing to undertake. The issues illuminated by examining Greece and Germany through a mythological lens are not exclusive to either nation. Sadly, they reflect problems many countries face, as does the dynamic between the two. Both money and psychological complexes reside in the space in between. In terms of money, someone owes while someone else is owed. Complexes often function as bipolar systems, indicating an interplay between two complexes, such as mother and child or senex and puer (Perry, 1970). This seems to hold true for Germany and Greece.

Street art called *The Kiss of Discord* by the world-famous Jupiterfab illustrated this interplay between Greece and Germany by showing an image of the Greek Prime Minister, Alexis Tsipras, about to kiss the German Chancellor Angel Merkel. It is on a building in the neighborhood of Psirri in Athens, home of locals and immigrants who particularly felt the impact of the crisis and austerity measures.

The Meeting of the Complexes: A Mythic View

The film *Highway to Hellas* (Beckmann et al., 2015) shows the shadow play between Greece and Germany. Jorge, a German banker, travels to a small Greek island to ensure the bank's loan is used to develop infrastructure, including an electric plant, a hospital, and a wildlife sanctuary. The Greek people tried to trick Jorge into thinking they had used the funds as promised, which was only partially true. However, it unfolds that the German bank wanted the Greeks to default on their loans so the bank could take over their beaches and build hotels to save themselves. It demonstrated the continuation of neocolonialism.

Greece and Germany's cultural complexes evoke images of long-standing archetypal dyads such as North vs South, spirit vs. soul, civilization vs. instinctual. These dyads are reflected in the mythic figures the Titans and Dionysus, Apollo and Dionysus, and the senex-puer. They are also seen in the geography: Germany is North, while Greece is Europe's southernmost country. Germany has long, cold winters, while Greece has extended, hot summers. Greece is small and surrounded by water, while Germany is large and mainly landlocked.

Hillman (1983) noted that most psychologies have their foundations in Europe's North which is "Aryan, Apollonic, Germanic, positivistic, voluntaristic, rationalistic, Cartesian, protestant, scientistic, personalistic, monotheistic, etc." (p. 31). This contrasts the sensuality and concreteness of the South with its Mediterranean gods and goddesses, who do not view the soul from a "northern moralistic perspective" (p. 31).

The South is often considered the "other" to the North. The Global South is often perceived as "less than" the North and is viewed as a source of cheap raw materials for the industrialized North and a market for their products. The South embodies what has been repressed and considered inferior (Barcellos, 2012, pp. 24–25). This includes pleasure, beauty, the body, lust, instinct, joy, the Dionysian, paganism, the feminine, and Nature. Germany may have a superiority complex, and Greece and the Mediterranean seem to suffer from an inferiority complex. Barcellos argues that the South and soul need to be reimagined so that they are not seen as the "other" to the North, but instead they are brought into balance. This would bring in many elements left out of our current economic system, such as the feminine, Nature, community, and relationships. This would help to counter neocolonialism.

The tensions between the North and South are seen in the mythic duo of Apollo and Dionysus. Jung and other scholars noted the opposition and tension between Apollo and Dionysus, yet both are needed. Apollo is concerned with the spirit, while Dionysus is the Lord of Souls, "the vitality of life itself" (Hillman, 2007, p. 147). Dionysian consciousness is emotional and experiential and grants proximity, while Apollo's consciousness is formal and abstract and allows us distance (Paris, 1990). If a culture is all about Apollonian light, then "it dries up and dies," and if there is too much moisture from Dionysus, "it rots and becomes crazy" (p. 10). Both Apollo and Dionysus were present at the economic center of Ancient Delphi. Apollo was the leader. However, Dionysus had a presence, too. In one of the rituals at Delphi, Apollo buried the heart of the dismembered Dionysus near the sacred tripod.

Perhaps Greece and Germany fell into the unconscious role of balancing each other out, as Dionysus and Apollo balance each other. A better option would be for both countries to engage with the Apollonian and the Dionysian rather than repress and project their undesired aspects. This would entail

Dionysus's return not just to the dominant players in capitalism, such as Germany and the North, but also a deep Greek engagement with all of Dionysus and the sacrifice he required.

Hillman (1972) argued that by allowing Dionysian consciousness to enter us, digressions, descents, and depression are less pathologized, and there is less focus on the heroic consciousness concerned with upward progress (p. 284). By bringing Dionysus into economics, we may become less concerned with increases in GDP and the ups and downs of economic cycles. Dionysus can also undo Midas's curse. Dionysus granted Midas's wish to have everything he touched turn gold. He also ended it by telling Midas to dive into the river Pactolos. This washing away in the water undid the golden touch and left the river rich with gold. The emergence into water, often considered an image of the unconscious and a metaphor for rebirth, is the panacea for the destruction of greed and the golden touch.

Greece and Germany must pull back their projections and engage with their shadows. Germany must sacrifice its superior and responsible attitude and recognize its shadowy elements. Greece needs to sacrifice its identification with Dionysus, acknowledge its own Titanic elements, and re-engage with the fullness of Dionysus. It also seems to go without saying that all parties need to acknowledge and continue to address the inherent problems in capitalism and the EU's structure. This is critical because the leading players that have been discussed—the U.S., Greece, and Germany—seemed to have lost touch with the instinctual elements of humanity in their self-perceptions of being divine and pure.

In retaliation for their violence against Dionysus, Zeus struck the Titans with lightning, reducing them to ashes from which humans were created. The ashes of the consumed Dionysus and the charred Titans reflect the duality of humanity as both divine and something less godly (Lopez-Pedraza, 2000). These less godly aspects of humanity must be confronted. Jung emphasized the role of instincts in human life, reminding us that we are part of the natural, animal world, with biological drives that can become problematic if they are not transformed or contained. Christianity's emphasis on denying and repressing these instincts or projecting them onto the devil prevents their integration, allowing them to run rampant on Wall Street and in governments. Greece's red thread led me to consider the significant impact of a group's God-image on its economic health.

References

Barcellos, G. (2012). South and the soul. In P. Amezaga, G. Barcellos, A. Capriles, J. Gerson, & D. Ramos (Eds.), *Listening to Latin America: Exploring cultural complexes in Brazil, Chile, Colombia, Mexico, Uruguay, and Venezuela* (pp. 17–30). Spring Journals, Inc.

Beaton, R. (2019). *Greece: Biography of a modern nation*. Allen Lane.

Beckmann, M., Geike, W., Happ, S., Maag, D., Maag, H. Schimkat, A., … & Lehmann, A.. (2015). *Highway to Hellas* [Motion picture]. Pantaleon Films.

Butler, E. M. (1935). *The tyranny of Greece over Germany*. Cambridge University Press.

Dimou, N. (2015, March 21). The bailout crisis: Why Greece is content to put the blame on Germany. *The Guardian*. Retrieved from https://www.theguardian.com/world/commentisfree/2015/mar/22/greece-scapegoats-germany-eurozone-crisis

Germany Made Billions on Greece's Debt Crisis, Berlin Confirms. (2018, June 21). *The Local*. Retrieved from https://www.thelocal.de/20180621/germany-made-billions-on-greeces-debt-crisis-berlin-confirms

Henderson, J. L. (Ed.). (1990). The cultural unconscious. In *Shadow and self: Selected papers in analytical psychology* (pp. 103–113). Chiron.

Hillman, J. (1972). *The myth of analysis*. Northwestern University Press.

Hillman, J. (1976). *Re-visioning psychology*. Harper & Row.

Hillman, J. (1983). *Archetypal psychology: A brief account*. Spring Publications, Inc.

Hillman, J. (2007). *Mythic figures*. Spring Publications, Inc.

Hillman, J. (n.d.). *Culture and the animal soul*. Retrieved from https://www.malintzin.org/attachments/029_Hillman%20-%20Culture%20and%20the%20Animal%20Soul.pdf

Jung, C. G. (1969a). General aspects of dream psychology (R. F. C. Hull, Trans.). In H. Read et al. (Eds.), *The collected works of C.G. Jung* (Vol. 8, 2nd ed., pp. 237–280). Princeton University Press (Original work published 1916).

Jung, C. G. (1969b). A review of the complex theory (R. F. C. Hull, Trans.). In H. Read et al. (Eds.), *The collected works of C.G. Jung* (Vol. 8, 2nd ed., pp. 92–106). Princeton University Press (Original work published 1948).

Jung, C. G. (1969c). Aion: Researches into the phenomenology of the self (R. F. C. Hull, Trans.). In H. Read et al. (Eds.), *The collected works of C.G. Jung* (Vol. 9 pt. 2, 2nd ed.). Princeton University Press (Original work published 1951).

Lopez-Pedraza, R. (2000). *Dionysus in exile: On the reprisal of the body and emotion*. Chiron Publications.

Palaiologos, Y. (2015). *The 13th labour of Hercules: Inside the Greek crisis*. Portobello Books.

Paris, G. (1990). *Pagan grace: Dionysos, Hermes, and Goddess Memory in daily life*. Spring Publications.

Perry, J. W. (1970). Emotions and object relations. *Journal of Analytical Psychology*, *15*(1), 1–13.

Rasche, J. (2016). Introduction. In J. Rasche & T. Singer (Eds.), *Europe's many souls: Exploring cultural complexes and identities* (pp. 15–31). Spring Journal, Inc.

Sauer, G. (2016). About two cultural complexes. In J. Rasche & T. Singer (Eds.), *Europe's many souls: Exploring cultural complexes and identities* (pp. 211–234). Spring Journal.

Schenk, R. (2012). *American soul: A cultural narrative*. Spring Journal Books.

Seiradaki, E. (2012, April 5). Schaeuble on CBS: Germany is Greece's scapegoat. *Greek Reporter*. Retrieved from https://greece.greekreporter.com/2012/04/05/schaeuble-on-cbs-germany-is-greeces-scapegoat/

Singer, T. (2011). Preface. In C. San Rogue, A. Dowd, & D. Tacey (Eds.), *Placing psyche: Exploring cultural complexes in Australia* (pp. xii–xvi). Spring Journal, Inc.

Singer, T. (2014). Psyche and society: Some personal reflections on the development of the cultural complex theory. *Journal of Jungian Scholarly Studies*, *9*(1), 1–12.

Singer, T. (2016). Introduction. In J. Rasche & T. Singer (Eds.), *Europe's many souls: Exploring cultural complexes and identities* (pp. 1–14). Spring Books, Inc.

Singer, T. (2020). Introduction. In T. Singer (Ed.), *Cultural complexes and the soul of America: Myth, psyche, and politics*. Routledge.

Smith, R. (2018). This country works the longest hours in Europe. Retrieved from https://www.weforum.org/agenda/2018/02/greeks-work-longest-hours-in-europe/

Snow, J. (2012, February 20). *Channel 4 News* [Television Broadcast]. Retrieved from https://www.youtube.com/watch?v=KwY89ZuQWdc

Tsempelis, E. (2019). Greek nihilism and the psychology of decadence. In T. Singer, J. Cashford, & C. San Roque (Eds.), *When the soul remembers itself: Ancient Greece, Modern Psyche* (pp. 189–213). Routledge.

7 A God's View

I was surprised that Greece led me down a religious path while exploring the Global Financial Crisis. Before spending time in Greece, my idea of a Greek God brought up images of ancient pagan gods and goddesses. However, I quickly learned that modern Greece is dominated by one God, the patriarchal God of Eastern Orthodox Christianity. The Greek Orthodox Church plays a significant role in modern Greece, reflected in the thousands of churches that dot the land and the Church's deep ties to the government. The Church is an integral part of the educational system and "has long been not just a religious force but also an economic one, with a stake in the Greek National Bank, landholdings second only to the Greek government and a clergy bankrolled by the state" (Birnbaum, 2012, para. 2).

As noted in Chapter 3, many experts have argued that the Church has been problematic for Greece's economic condition. Given this and the discussions in Chapter 2 about the connections between religion and money and the discussions in Chapter 7 about the relationship between cultural complexes and religion in the U.S., Germany, and Greece, it makes sense to examine the God-images in the Global Financial Crisis. It is also relevant to discuss the God-image in the context of Jung because he and many other depth psychologists recognized the importance of spirituality on mental health and the relationship between the God-image and the psyche.

A Depth Psychological View of God

Depth psychology is less focused on theoretical discussions about the nature of God and more interested in the idea that "'God' is a psychological fact" (Corbett, 1996, p. 39). That is not to say that depth psychology is not concerned with the essence of the divine. Jung's ideas about the soul and Self certainly dive into theological thought; however, Jung was more concerned with people's personal experiences of God.

Jung believed the psyche was religious by nature and that people, individually and collectively, hold culturally influenced images of God, which contain projected aspects of the Self. We project parts of our own divinity onto

DOI: 10.4324/9781003497622-7

the Gods. The God-image does not necessarily reflect religious teachings. Instead, it reflects whatever is of the highest importance—consciously and unconsciously—in the psyche: "This may be money, science, power, sex, or wherever a person becomes absolute" (Corbett, 2013, p. 5). A group's image of God impacts its values and behaviors and what it worships in its churches and its secular lives. It also influences a group's perceptions about its role in this world and the powers that people and the divine hold.

The God-image plays a significant role in shaping people's everyday experiences, including their economic activities. Analyzing the God-image in the context of economics is not about evaluating the accuracy of religious beliefs regarding a higher power. Instead, it focuses on what a community's perception of God reveals about its collective outlook and how it affects its economic behaviors. To improve economic conditions, we must transform the current God-image—not just in our religious institutions but also in our nations, governments, organizations, and communities.

In many religious traditions, God is understood through doctrines and teachings by spiritual leaders. In depth psychology, the inner knowledge of the Holy is based on personal experiences. The experience of the God-image is not transcendent; instead, it is subjective and relative and reveals aspects of the unconscious. Jung used the term religion not in the context of established dogmas and creeds. Instead, he took it back to its original meaning of the numinosum, "a dynamic agency or effect not caused by an arbitrary act of will" (1940/1969, para. 6). Meaning people have involuntary, spontaneous experiences of the divine that are mysterious and remarkable. They can take many forms, such as experiencing the sacred in dreams, Nature, or a synchronicity. Each person experiences the holy in their own way; "A numinous experience allows us to discover our authentic spirituality by giving us a *personal* symbol of the sacred, in contrast to collective symbols such as the cross" (Corbett, 2007, p. 14). Numinous experiences usually facilitate a direct experience of the archetypes, which can produce a healing effect and provide a sense of life but can also be overwhelming and frightening. They also challenge the ego because they are a reminder that it is not in control.

Some depth psychologists believe in a co-creation between the divine and humans, that "human beings act as a reflecting consciousness for divinity itself" (Corbett, 2013, p. 36). The sacred and people have a reciprocal relationship and contribute to the conscious development of each other; the individual "can be understood as a function of God, and God as a psychological function of man" (Jung, 1971, para. 412).

Examining a group's God-image is critical because it continues to uncover the cultural unconscious. Jung (1940/1969) argued that "every religion is a spontaneous expression of a certain predominant psychological condition" (para. 160). Considering the God-images in economics is critical to understanding the workings of the economic system. Although a group's God-image is not solely based on its religious teachings, it is a good starting point for uncovering the God-image.

The prominent players in the Global Financial Crisis—the U.S., Greece, and Germany—are strong Christian nations. Spain, Ireland, and Portugal, which were also profoundly impacted during the crisis, are also mainly Christian nations. Thus, it seems sensible to begin by looking at Christianity while appreciating its many variations, especially the differences between Eastern and Western Christianity.

Jung and many post-Jungians have recognized the spiritual potential of Christianity but also pointed out its problematic aspects. Like the field of economics, religious institutions are influenced by humans' fallibilities, thus disrupting the presence of the divine. Our God-images are formed at least partially by our desire to connect to and understand the divine; hence, in exploring the issues with Christianity, it is essential not to throw the baby Jesus out with the bathwater. Instead, we must examine and address where our humanness has interrupted our connection to the sacred.

A Depth Psychological View of the Problems with Christianity

Jung argued that Christianity lost the healing energies of myth and the symbolic world and its ability to help make people's lives more whole because of "a purely rationalistic approach to its role as mediator of the World of God" (Dourley, 1984, p. 14). Religion became something "out there" in the literalized written word instead of something experienced within the psyche.

Along with a rationality issue, Jung argued that Christianity suffers from too much light, masculinity, and spirit (Dourley, 1984). Jung noted that Christ has become a one-dimensional image seen as all good, emphasizing perfection instead of wholeness. The shadow aspects, including the feminine, instinctual, bodily, emotional, and intuitive, have been cut off and projected onto the devil, or Dionysus, as discussed in the previous chapter. Part of the problem of cutting people off from their instincts is that it leaves them to run amok in the shadows, as seen in religious institutions and the business world worldwide.

Instincts cannot be prayed away. The God-image needs to enable their transformation, which is a critical part of the process of individuation. The less savory aspects of humankind will continue to run the world from the shadows until we have a God-image that facilitates facing and integrating them and containing any that cannot be transformed.

The Church's focus on the Triune god, the Father, Son, and Spirit, is an exclusively masculine version of the divine. The feminine is limited to the Virgin Mary, who contains many positive attributes, including being kind, caring, and a good mother. However, she is one-dimensional and not particularly strong or independent (Woodman & Dickson, 1996). Woodman and Dickson argued that the shadow side of the Virgin Mary causes damage to women by putting immense pressure on them to be perfect and to sacrifice their needs to serve others. In ancient times, the word Virgin was not used in terms of chastity. Instead, it referred to women being whole in and of themselves and not needing a man. The powerful feminine, embodied in the apostle of the apostles, Mary Magdalene, and the pagan goddesses, has been relegated to the shadows.

Depth psychologists also pointed out the dominance of the spirit and senex in Christianity, which, in turn, causes a soul problem. Hillman (2005) argued that the Western image of God is

> Omniscient, omnipotent, eternal, seated and bearded, a ruler through abstract principle of justice, morality, and order, a faith in words yet not given to self-explanation in speech, benevolent but enraged when his will is crossed, removed from the feminine (wifeless) and the sexual aspect of creation, up high with a geometric world of stars and planets in the cold and distant night of numbers.
>
> (p. 252)

Christianity has lost connection to the Earth, the feminine, and soul. Mogenson (2005) argued that religions frequently focus on what God demands rather than on what the soul wants: "'God first, psyche second'" (p. 10).

The God-image is also connected to trauma, which clearly impacts a community's well-being, including their economic lives. People's traumas become gods; "The psychological fact remains that we tend to experience traumatic events *as if* they were in some sense divine" and "the traumatic event seems infinite, all-powerful, and wholly other" (Mogenson, 2005, p. 9). When trauma is explained as God's will, it makes God and his actions incomprehensible. This stops the creation of images that absorb and transform deep emotions and trauma; it "dislocates the mediating function of the imagination" (p. 51). The person can remain stuck in the trauma, and the connection to the imagination continues to erode. However, "any god that takes the imagination captive is not a god at all" (p. 97). Trauma may be one of the foundational reasons for the original rise of Christianity. Stark (1997) noted the impact of disease epidemics and deadly disasters on the desire for a God-image that could help explain why so many people were dying and provide hope for an afterlife and immortality. These were found more readily in Christianity.

The image of God based on trauma often creates a dependency on the higher power that requires compliance with His will. People remain children to an all-powerful, often punishing God, leaving them with a limited sense of agency to co-create with the divine. Mogenson (2005) pointed out that we lose our connection to soul through identifying with either the human perspective or the God perspective, both of which lead to unconsciousness "on the one hand, we lose soul to the human-all-too-human and, on the other, to a God before whom one may have no other 'as if' structures" (p. 13). People may put all their power in His hands. However, the opposite can also be true. Some people believe that power lies in human hands; there is no god to contend with. This hubris and abandonment of the gods is readily seen in Silicon Valley and on Wall Street.

Christianity also appears to have a suffering problem. Emphasizing the story of Christ's crucifixion and salvation creates a God who is "angry and needs to be appeased" and makes "suffering a prerequisite for having a relationship with God" (Corbett, 2007, p. 138). However, "not every wound is a crucifixion" (Mogenson, 2005, p. 17). Other forms of suffering can be more productive. Hillman (1983) noted that:

> Christianity has nailed suffering to resurrection—first nail: it is good for you; second nail; it is isolating and heroic, and third, it always leads to a better day, Easter. Well, it doesn't—we all know that! Suffering has other models, too, like deepening in the sense of Saturn, like dissolving and letting go in the sense of Dionysus, like raging and fighting back; it can make for prophesy; it can make for love; or the kinds of suffering we see in the women in Greek drama. We need many models, besides the Christian one, to locate our psychological experiences.
>
> (p. 76)

What we need is "salvation from the very notion of salvation itself" (Mogenson, 2005, p. 107). Mogenson argued for the need for post-Christian art to "provide a container for events and experiences which might otherwise prove unabsorbable" (p. 104). New images are required to help in dealing with trauma and its subsequent impact on people's economic lives. Ideally, ones that include the instinctual, the feminine, and Nature. As explored extensively in Chapter 4, the Western God-image separates people from Nature. Made in the image of God, man is seen as superior to Nature, which is not true in the religions of other places and times.

A new God-image must dim Christ's light and recognize the significance of our instinctual lives. This acknowledgment of our connection to the natural world will help in the reconnection to Nature and curtail the power and greed that run amok in our economic worlds. Jung wrote extensively about the need to integrate these shadow aspects in his work on alchemy. The new God-image should return us to soul and the symbolic life; "so bankrupt have we become by the worship of our old God that we require a new God to bail us out" (Mogenson, 2005, p. 53).

The God-Image in the Global Financial Crisis

A new God-image is needed to continue to address the problems of the Global Financial Crisis, particularly the divine child and purity problem, which Greece, Germany, and the U.S. all seem to suffer from. The nations' focus on their own divinity stops them from recognizing the holiness of other places and peoples. It also hinders them from recognizing where they contribute to their own or other nations' problems. As discussed in Chapter 4, this also perpetuates a monolithic approach to economics because the nuances of places are not valued. What if each country were not wrapped up in a sense of specialness but instead were open to seeing the specialness in others? This is the true diversity that the goddess Themis facilitates.

This image of God-the-father creates the potential for a father complex in which people find "that teachers, coaches, ministers, policemen, or his superior officers in the army gall him unaccountably, the moment he perceives in them any assertion of positive mastery" (Perry, 1970, para. 15). The person may take on the role of the rebellious son, becoming "petulant and querulous and suddenly appears more youthful and inept than one would expect from his customary demeanor" (para. 15). We see this father complex in the resistance to any government authority, even that which supports economic, environmental, and psychological health. This father-son complex keeps the individual from achieving maturity. However, it also provides an opportunity to achieve adulthood through working with the complex.

God-images with a focus on the Virgin Mary can leave people with a mother complex. Mary's role as a continual sacrificer and giver leaves people puerile as continual, dependent receivers. They can take whatever they want from Mother Nature; she is there solely for their benefit. It also takes the puer further from the wisdom of the positive senex and his beneficial limitations (Hillman, 2005, p. 123).

The U.S. God in the Crisis

As noted, the God-image is not just found in the teachings of religious institutions but is whatever is of the highest importance in the psyche. The U.S. has religious diversity, although it is heavily Christian, making many of the depth psychological critiques about Christianity relevant. It is worth discussing more extensively how the Virgin Mary may work against the feminine and women in economic health. Woodman and Dickson's insights about how the role model of the Virgin Mary restricts women are reflected in the concept of benevolent sexism developed by the sociologists Glick and Fiske (1996). Benevolent sexism, or BS as I like to call it, is a form of gender bias that seems positive but reflects stereotyped and traditional gender roles, such as "Women have a quality of purity that few men possess" (Glick & Fiske, 1996, p. 500). Benevolent sexism reinforces beliefs that men and women are different, that women should play a supporting role to men, and that women need men's protection. All of which reinforces the importance of the masculine and diminishes the power and autonomy of the feminine. It begs the questions: If God does not value women and men equally, why should people, and why should organizations pay them equally?

Benevolent Sexism is a subtle yet powerful way of wielding power. Research has shown that benevolent sexism has a more negative impact on women's motivation and self-esteem than does the more typical hostile sexism, which consists of antagonistic attitudes toward women (Glick, 2013). Women seem to know how to fight direct sexism but are unsure of what to do with the BS's disguised flattery. Perhaps the most concerning thing is that in many cultures, women are just as likely to hold benevolent sexist attitudes as men. Women internalize the beliefs they have been exposed to over their lifetime and are unaware that they lie in their unconscious. Benevolent sexism also contributes to cutting women off from the instincts and the body, perpetuating the Madonna/whore narrative. Benevolent sexism must be addressed to bring the full feminine back into the economic system.

The feminine and Nature are not of the highest importance in the U.S.'s image of God. Instead, it worships the Titans' money and power, which are found on Wall Street and in business; "the market itself is in the position of godlike power," and the nation's soul is its capitalistic economy (Schenk, 2012, p. 166). The belief that successful businesspeople, particularly technology mavens, are divine and should have power over people's lives can be seen in the business Titans' involvement in politics.

The U.S. worships freedom from government control, taxes, and financial and gun regulation. Despite Christian teachings about people being responsible for caring for each other's well-being, the U.S.'s God-image encourages a focus on the individual. The U.S. also worships the unbridled innovation of Silicon Valley. Technological development answers to no god except perhaps the venture capitalists. Progress and profits are more important than adolescent health. The power lies in human hands, as seen in the Titan Prometheus, who stole fire from the Olympian gods. Slater (2024) argued that to be Promethean "is to forge ahead with willful abandon and inventive cunning, an approach that risks the wrath of the gods" (p. 54).

The Greek Orthodox God in the Crisis

Many of depth psychology's criticisms of Christianity also apply to the Greek Orthodox Church, which was "cemented" to the Greek state by the Greek War of Independence and plays a large part in the Greek identity. Noting Greece's placement bordering the east and west, Dimou (2015) argued that Greece is not a typical European nation and "belongs to an entirely different civilization: the Orthodox one, together with Serbia and Russia" (para. 14).

It is interesting to note that over the years, immigrants brought the Orthodox Church to the U.S., and the largest English-speaking Russian Orthodox monastery in the world is in West Virginia (Yousef, 2022). Although a very small part of the U.S. population, there is evidence of growing converts to the Orthodox religion seeking its more conservative views. There is some concern that some extremists are trying to distort the Church to support the far-right.

After working extensively with the Orthodox Church, Markides (2008) argued that the Orthodox religion holds promise in the re-enchantment of Western culture and that it contains "spiritual jewels lying dormant" (p.196). Elements of the three distinct stages that people must go through to reunite with God—Catharsis, Fortisis, and Theosis—align in some ways with Jungian thought. For instance, the ego and its desires need to be kept in check, and recognizing our own divine nature is essential. However, as with many organized religions, the Church "needs to be freed from its limited and homogenous cultural milieu" and "come to terms with the western enlightenment and modern critical thought" (pp. 195–196). As an Orthodox religion, it is conservative and "traditionally an enemy of modernization (especially if it meant a relegation of its role in education and social life or its separation from the state and the generous funding it receives from it) and deeply suspicious of Western influence" (Palaiologos, 2015, p. 16). The Church has also been criticized for its tax breaks and relationships with political leaders, which were "starving the country of revenue at a moment when time and money are running short" (Birnbaum, 2012, para. 3).

As explored in Chapter 3, many of the crisis experts criticized the Church's impact on the economic lives of the Greeks, although they appreciated how it fed the poor during the crisis. A sociologist, Kessareas (2018), analyzed how Greek Orthodox fundamentalists explained the causes and remedies of the crisis. Looking at this more extreme population uncovers aspects of the Greek God-image if their views are approached as if they amplify the more moderate approach, which helps to get a clearer view of what is happening in the cultural unconscious. The Church leaders' narrative is that the Greek people and the Orthodox Church are persecuted heroes fighting for freedom against their archenemies, foreigners, and atheists "who once more attempt to enslave the Greeks, this time by elaborate financial means" (p. 127). The enemies plan to de-Christianize Greece and, in doing so, "rid it of its spiritual uniqueness, disabling it from fulfilling its unique historical destiny" (p. 128). Images of a shadowless divine child emerge again.

The Church leaders blamed the "abandonment of traditional values of fatherland, faith and family" and the pursuit of the secularized Western world for causing the crisis (Kessareas, 2018, p. 125). They also used collective guilt by aligning themselves with the criticisms of the rest of the world, accusing the Greek people and government of causing the crisis because they were corrupt, hedonistic, and lazy. Even those who were not corrupt were responsible because "they have the same mentality as the others, and they would have done the same in their position" (p. 130). People are told to be "indignant with ourselves," and instead of protesting against the political system, the people should be going to the confessionals (p. 131).

The Church leaders divide spirituality and wealth: "Austerity and even the condition of poverty were framed as the genuine Orthodox road to salvation in contrast to wealth, consumerism and materialism" (Kessareas, 2018, p. 130).

The Orthodox God also requires sacrifice, as God "always rewards the faithful Greek nation for its patience and sacrifices" and its need to take the bitter medicine (p. 132). Pushing back on the focus on materialism and the need to sacrifice are tremendously important in the fight against the Titans. However, the message also widens the split between money and soul. The focus on austerity, salvation, and the rejection of the material world can lead to a neglect of the soulful elements of human life.

The Church leaders advocated fixing the crisis through an attitude of repentance and returning to the traditional ways of the Church or "full steam backward" (Kessareas, 2018, p. 127). The Church only condones a fighting spirit that protects Orthodox values: "It is clearly rejected when it aims at the radical transformation of the established system" (p. 133). There seems to be little chance of imagining something new. The Church leader's pronouncements of the crisis as punishment and demands that the Greek people follow His will and return to old ways may leave the Greek people feeling little agency to co-create with Him.

The inability to create change may also be seen in the Church's static, enigmatic, and somber icons of divine figures and events such as saints, Christ, the Virgin Mary, and the Crucifixion and Resurrection. These icons are found in churches, homes, and businesses to protect their inhabitants. They are considered written rather than painted because they convey aspects of Orthodox doctrine. Exhibits at The Byzantine and Christian Museum highlight the time of iconoclasm and the Church's victory in retaining its icons because of their connection to the Holy. Hillman (2005), however, did not find it a win, arguing that by venerating images instead of creating and adoring them, images become allegories, and "when images become allegories, the iconoclasts have won" (p. 73). This means that when images are only seen to point to something divine or holy rather than being recognized as sacred themselves, they lose their power. For Jung, psyche is image, which involves spontaneous symbol formation and a connection to the unconscious and soul. Despite Hillman's concerns, I, like some others, find something numinous in the Orthodox icons while also appreciating the need for the ability for images to emerge and evolve.

Hillman (2007) argued that "instinct and image *are* each other" (p. 210). Repressing one represses the other. The Church's icons focus on two dimensions rather than three, which brings in the physical world, may also emphasize spirit at the expense of soul. Hillman (2005) argued that this Byzantine victory ended up splitting mind (spirit) from body (matter) and left the world without soul. It was the "victory of our tradition of spirit over soul" (p. 73). Greece's most holy time, Easter, and its attention to eternal life also reflect the priority of spirit over soul.

The Holy Passion is significant in Greek culture, connecting to its traumatic history. Jesus's journey has been likened to the hero's journey. However, as noted above, limiting the image of suffering to the Passion prohibits the power of other forms of suffering and transformation. We can get stuck in our suffering, believing it to be the only way to salvation. A different image may help to metabolize trauma and find a new way forward.

The Orthodox way creates an image of an unchanging church with a static God, preventing evolution. We find ourselves back in the world of the senex. Church leaders' pronouncements of the crisis as punishment and a demand to return to old ways may stop the Greek people from making meaning of the crisis. The punishing, all-powerful Greek God-image whose will is to be followed may leave the Greek people dependent and with little agency to co-create with Him. The conservative, self-righteous, moral senex eats his own children and "its own possibilities of change" (Hillman, 2005, p. 44). Developing a relationship of co-creation, rather than one of parent and child, may help increase a sense of agency and accountability.

The powerful feminine is not fully realized in the Greek Orthodox Church. Women do not hold leadership roles and are banned from Mount Athos, the holiest place of the Greek Orthodox Church. This may reflect the masculine domination in Greece, which has some of the lowest gender equality ratings in Europe (European Institute for Gender Equality, 2019). Nikolaos (2008), a scientist from MIT and Harvard and a senior official in the Greek Orthodox Church in Athens, argued that "the basic function of the female body to which the entire female existence is directed is the reproductive function. The woman exists anatomically, physiologically and sentimentally for the embryo, the pregnancy, and childbearing" (p. 26), confining women to traditional roles and without a connection to the instinctual and sexual realm.

I experienced this repression of a more empowered and whole feminine on a guided tour to Corinth, the home of Aphrodite, the goddess of beauty, sensuality, love, and fertility with connections to Nature and passion. I had hoped to visit her temple; however, the tour focused on the Christian story of Paul speaking to the Corinthians, and Aphrodite was only a footnote. Aphrodite seems to be missing from the Orthodox Church, as do Demeter and Persephone, goddesses of the harvest and soul, who, in ancient times, were firmly contained in the ancients' image of God.

A rigid God-image can only hold so much energy, so the repressed life force is often expressed in secular gods, like the government. The crisis experts noted that the Greek government has also proven to resist change and is overly focused on rules and hierarchy. This has harmed economic activity, particularly entrepreneurship. The experts also argued that the people see the government as corrupt and unconcerned with their welfare and thus feel the need to fight and resist the government. Despite this resistance, there also seems to be a sense of dependence or an expectation to be taken care of, as there is a desire for government employment and an expectation of generous pensions and tax breaks. Thus, the Greeks have a conflicting relationship with the government, in which the government is untrustworthy and needs to be resisted yet also depended upon. Perhaps some of their repressed frustrations with the Church and its teachings play out in their relationship with the government, which seems to be a fair target for their anger.

This deeper dive into the cultural unconscious takes us further into the world of the negative senex and puer, who seem to lumber our economic lives with their greediness, oppressiveness, and irresponsibility. Perhaps this is why Greece was so profoundly impacted during the crisis; it was the place of their collision. The senex deeply embedded in Greece's God-image has been forced to meet the puer of Western economics.

What is interesting is that the positive aspects of the senex and puer are critical to economic health. The puer brings in new energy, innovation, and change, which needs to be combined with the wisdom and guidance of the positive senex, the wise old man. Transforming the God-image to reunite the two, which Hillman (2005) argued can only be done with the feminine, would go a long way to rectifying the issues in our economic world and reuniting money and soul. Loosening the God-image petrified in trauma could bring back the imagination and the potential to find new images to help people deal with open wounds. People need a God-image that reconnects them to their instinctual lives and supports them in becoming whole. This requires a sacrifice of the identity as a divine child and an acknowledgment of the shadow. Addressing cultural wounds and transforming God-images feel like Herculean trials. Not surprisingly, Greece revealed how to face and overcome what feels impossible.

References

Birnbaum, M. (2012, May 30). In Greece, church's tangled ties with government raise questions. *The Washington Post*. Retrieved from https://www.washingtonpost.com/world/europe/in-greece-churchs-tangled-ties-with-government-raise-questions/2012/05/30/gJQAFySG1U_story.html

Corbett, L. (1996). *The religious function of the psyche*. Routledge.

Corbett, L. (2007). *Psyche and the sacred: Spirituality beyond religion*. Spring Journal Books.

Corbett, L. (2013). Jung's approach to spirituality and religion. In K. Pargament (Ed.), *APA handbook of psychology, religion, and spirituality* (Vol. 2, pp. 147–167). APA Press.

Dimou, N. (2015, March 21). The bailout crisis: Why Greece is content to put the blame on Germany. *The Guardian*. Retrieved from https://www.theguardian.com/world/commentisfree/2015/mar/22/greece-scapegoats-germany-eurozone-crisis

Dourley, J. P. (1984). *The illness that we are: A Jungian critique of Christianity*. Inner City Books.

European Institute for Gender Equality. (2019). *Gender equality index 2019: Greece* (PDF: MH-01-19-029-EN-N ISBN 978-92-9470-774-1 doi: 10.2839/211736). Retrieved from https://ec.europa.eu/greece/sites/greece/files/gender_equality_index_2019_greece.pdf

Glick, P. (2013, February). BS at work: How benevolent sexism undermines women and justifies backlash. In R. J. Ely & A. J. C. Cudd (Organizers), *Gender & work:*

Challenging conventional wisdom. Symposium conducted at Harvard Business School, Boston, MA.

Glick, P., & Fiske, S. T. (1996). The ambivalent sexism inventory: Differentiating hostile and benevolent sexism. *Journal of Personality and Social Psychology*, *70*(3), 491–512.

Hillman, J. (1983). *Inter views*. Harper & Row.

Hillman, J. (2005). *Senex & puer*. G. Slater (Ed.). Spring Publications.

Hillman, J. (2007). *Mythic figures*. Spring Publications, Inc.

Jung, C. G. (1969). Psychology and religion. In H. Read et al. (Eds.), *The collected works of C. G. Jung* (Vol. 11, 2nd ed., pp. 3–107). Princeton University Press (Original work published 1940).

Jung, C. G. (1971). The collected works of C. G. Jung: Vol. 6. Psychological types (R. F. C. Hull, Trans.). In H. Read et al. (Eds.), *The collected works of C.G. Jung*. Princeton University Press (Original work published 1921).

Kessareas, E. (2018). The Greek debt crisis as theodicy: Religious fundamentalism and sociopolitical conservatism. *The Sociological Review*, *66*(1), 122–137.

Markides, K. C. (2008). Eastern Orthodox mysticism and transpersonal theory. *The Journal of Transpersonal Psychology*, *40*(2), 178–198.

Mogenson, G. (2005). *A most accursed religion: When a trauma becomes God*. Spring Publications, Inc.

Nikolaos, M. (2008, November). The Greek Orthodox position on the ethics of assisted reproduction. *Ethics, Bioscience and Life*, *3*(3), 25–33.

Palaiologos, Y. (2015). *The 13th labour of Hercules: Inside the Greek crisis*. Portobello Books.

Perry, J. W. (1970). Emotions and object relations. *Journal of Analytical Psychology*, *15*(1), 1–13.

Schenk, R. (2012). *American soul: A cultural narrative*. Spring Journal Books.

Slater, G. (2024). *Jung vs. Borg: Finding the deeply human in a posthuman age*. Winter Press.

Stark, R. (1997). *The rise of Christianity: How the obscure, marginal Jesus movement became the dominant religious force in the western world in a few centuries*. HarperCollins.

Woodman, M., & Dickson, E. (1996). *Dancing in the flames: The dark goddess in the transformation of consciousness*. Shambhala Publications.

Yousef, O. (2022, May 10). Orthodox Christian churches are drawing in far-right American converts. *NPR*. Retrieved from https://www.npr.org/2022/05/10/1096741988/orthodox-christian-churches-are-drawing-in-far-right-american-converts

8 A Transformative View

So, where did the red thread take us on our journey through the labyrinth of the Global Financial Crisis? First, we encountered the anima mundi and the wisdom it offers if places are viewed symbolically. For instance, on Wall Street, the literal and metaphorical divisions between humans and the natural world are set in concrete. A healthy economic life requires acknowledging the world soul, a place's genius loci, and the interdependence of people and places. A worldview recognizing the necessity of working with Nature rather than exploiting it would significantly transform economic policy.

Second, when examining issues in the U.S. and Greece through a trauma lens, cultural elements impeding economic health appear to reflect unhealed collective suffering. These open wounds often trace back to the nations' foundations. These complex aspects, including defense mechanisms and rigid identities, cannot be addressed through criticism or logic alone. Instead, they must be engaged in the realm of imagination, which will be explored further in this chapter.

Third, the red thread led us into the territory of complexes and the shadow, supporting Jung's insights that we often first see our shadow in the face of our neighbor. As challenging as it may be, confronting the shadow is essential for psychological and cultural development. Johnson (1986) observed that "if you repress a part of yourself and keep it out of your conscious life, it turns into a robber and starts 'stealing' your time and energy by creating a neurosis" (p. 120). The shadowy aspects of Greek, German, and U.S. cultures appear to be siphoning away crucial time and energy, potentially jeopardizing a healthy future. Ironically, this also deprives individuals of freedom because unaddressed complexes restrict people's ability to make conscious choices. Unconscious forces direct their lives.

Fourth, the red thread stressed the importance of considering how a community's God-image affects its socioeconomic life. The God-image reflects what is worshipped in people's churches and secular lives, shaping who holds economic power. The feminine holds little authority within the Christian God-image. Hestia and Themis are sorely missed. The Cartesian, Christian worldview eschews the Dionysian, leaving people disconnected from their

DOI: 10.4324/9781003497622-8

instinctual and Natural roots and leaving the less refined aspects controlling their lives from the shadows. Economic health requires a loosening and transformation of the God-image and an embracing of Dionysus.

Viewing the GFC through a mythological lens uncovered the monopoly the enormous Titanic holds on the economic system and the need for the other gods and goddesses to bring in cultural elements essential to psychological and economic health:

> A sign of the absence of the gods is hugeness, not merely the reign of quantity, but enormity as a quality…Whether presented in the images of multi-national organizations, polluted oceans, or vast climatic changes, hugeness is the signature of the absent god.
>
> (Hillman, 2007, p. 146)

The mythological lens provided a view of the friction between the senex and puer. This should not be surprising. Hillman (2005) argued that the current moment in history, the present kairos, is requiring individuals to contend with the psychological connections "between past and future, old and new, expressed archetypally as the polarity of the senex and puer" (p. 31). Perhaps the GFC and Greece's unique experience of the crisis represented the kairos for exposing the fault lines in economics. Using a mythological perspective also revealed other enduring, global, archetypal dyads, such as the North and South, spirit and soul, the Titans and Dionysus, and Apollo and Dionysus. Embracing these archetypal tensions may facilitate the transcendent function, which Jung believed was critical to the psychological process of individuation.

A Depth Psychological View of Transformation

Alchemy and the Transcendent Function

Jung argued that the ancient alchemists' attempt to transform lead into gold served as a metaphor for individuation. The various stages of alchemy mirror the phases of psychological growth and maturity. For instance, in alchemy, the *nigredo* represents a period of complete darkness and decomposition. In psychology, it signifies a dark night of the soul when a person confronts their shadow. Psychological alchemy involves releasing parts of the ego and reconnecting with lost elements of the unconscious. Just as alchemists sought gold from lead, individuals search for their psychological gold within their shadows. Alchemy also facilitates the transformation of instincts, reducing their harmful effects. Moreover, alchemy requires engaging the imagination, which Jung described as "a key that opens the door to the secret of the opus" (Jung, 1937/1968, para. 400).

The final stage of alchemy, known as the *conjunctio*, involves a union of what seem to be opposites, such as the senex and puer or the masculine and feminine, typically one arising from the conscious realm and the other from the unconscious realm. This process requires holding the tension between opposites. This dynamic permits the transcendent function, in which something new is created—often a new level of being and consciousness or a new, more balanced perspective. Miller (2004) suggested that the transcendent function is the "metaphorical third," a space "where the opposites sit in tension, vacillate, oscillate, and allow a shift in consciousness" (p. 128). The newly emerged third element, the new consciousness, is the alchemical fourth (p. 123).

As is often the case in the Jungian world, the transcendent function does not result from a rational exercise. Instead, it emerges as a spontaneous symbol uniting the two opposites. Jung advocated for the value of play and art in promoting psychological healing and the transcendent function: "Fantasy activity in the unconscious generates symbols—images, motifs, patterns—that allow the fusion of material that would otherwise remain polarized" (Miller, 2004, p. 46). Engaging with the creative instinct helps people to gain insight into the unconscious and their inner worlds.

Jung believed the psyche inherently draws people toward reconciling opposing forces and individuation. The transcendent function "has an autonomy of its own and will, without guidance from us, move the psychic energy toward some new attitude or breakthrough" (Miller, 2004, p. 135). However, Western civilization's emphasis on the rational and logical has hindered its ability to function (Miller, p. 21).

Jung highlighted the individual's experience of the transcendent function. However, the transcendent function is also needed on a group level to address long-standing issues and conflicts that lack a natural, rational solution, such as gun control and abortion (Miller, 2004, p. 134). The ancient Greeks understood the power of the transcendent function in the plot device *Deus ex Machina*, meaning "god from the machine." This term refers to the technique in which a god or goddess unexpectedly appears on stage, providing a surprise solution to the characters' seemingly insurmountable problem.

Encouraging the transcendent function is challenging in the social realm because there is no container for doing the work, as there is in a therapeutic relationship (Miller, 2004). It also requires an alchemical attitude, meaning people must maintain an open mind and move beyond the ego. Thus, despite their challenges, the archetypal dyads revealed in the Global Financial Crises like the senex and puer provide an opportunity for the transcendent function and a new, more conscious way of being.

Reuniting the Senex and Puer

Hillman argued that the problems of the negative senex and puer are seen throughout history, doing battle "on the world-political and social stage, underpinning profound rifts between rigid conservatism and freewheeling expression evident everywhere we turn" (Hillman, 2005, introduction by

Slater, p. xi). The senex and puer are actually one archetype that splits when it enters ego-consciousness (p. 38). The split leaves us with their negative aspects, which resist development (p. 52). A healthy economy requires the reconciliation of the senex and puer. The positive puer brings the spark of innovation, which requires the guidance and wisdom of the positive senex.

The reconciliation of the two also addresses historical trauma and cultural complexes. If history is dominated by the puer, people risk becoming anti-historical, sweeping it under the rug (Hillman, 2005). The solo senex allows history to become a permanent truth (Hillman). Both aspects are evident in the global crisis. The U.S. and Greece are locked into their founding narratives. The positive puer provides an imaginative and mythological perspective on historical events, making the intolerable tolerable.

The soul has the potential to hold the senex and puer polarities harmoniously. However, the ego's dominance often prevents the soul from being present enough to do so. The feminine is required to serve as the holding container to reconcile the senex and puer; "without a proper feminine vessel, we can gestate nothing, nourish nothing, bring nothing to complete birth" (Hillman, 2005, p. 229). Greece provided guidance on embracing the soul and the feminine and showed signs of "playing" with the senex and puer in hopes of reuniting them, which will be discussed in a moment.

Shadow and Wound Work

Greece, Germany, and the U.S. all demonstrated the need to confront the shadow and address cultural wounds for economic health. Real heroes go into the shadows rather than project their own failings onto others. Meaningful, conscious, emotional suffering is also required to find freedom from the unconscious influences of unhealed wounds. This raises the question of how suffering, shadow-work, and healing can be done on a group level, particularly in cases where justice will not or cannot be served.

Trousdell's (2011) analysis of Aeschylus's play, *The Oresteia,* offers valuable insights. *The Oresteia* is the story of a long cycle of trauma and vengeance and has the first trial by jury. The protagonist, Orestes, is pursued by the dreaded Furies, the deities of vengeance, after he commits matricide in retaliation for his mother killing his father, an act she undertook because Orestes's father killed their daughter. Thus, like many cultural complexes, there were generations of wounding. Although Apollo puts the Furies to sleep, the ghost of Orestes's mother rouses them. Psychologically, our rational side can suppress our wounds, yet it only takes a single ghostly image of past offenses to reawaken the emotions.

When the Furies put Orestes on trial for killing his mother, Athena comes to his rescue. The jury is divided, and Athena casts the tie-breaking vote to acquit him, infuriating the Furies. She placates them by promising them a place in Athens where they will be honored yet contained. The Furies receive new robes to wear, and they gradually begin to stand upright, transforming into the kindly Eumenides. In doing all this, Athena provided a way to acknowledge the Furies, just as our wounds need a conscious place in the psyche. She also halts the pursuit of vengeance, which would have perpetuated the cycle of destruction like cultural complexes undermine economic health. This is a crucial part of healing a complex, which involves recognizing and holding a contained space for the wound without fixating on retribution that may never come (Trousdell, 2011). This shifts the energy from a quest for heroic vengeance or a stuckness in suffering and redirects it toward progressing in life. This process may also involve forming a new identity or at least loosening the grip of the old one. Both the U.S. and Greece could do with redefining themselves beyond the hero.

Trousdell (2011) pointed out that trauma needs to be worked with symbolically to address it. During the crisis, the Greek people seemed to understand the need to engage the symbolic world and to foster an environment for the transcendent function, or *deux ex machina*, to save the day. Throughout the crisis, but particularly toward the end, various cultural and art events in Greece worked to cultivate economic and psychological health. It was as if Greece was striving toward becoming a true hero through confronting the shadow and defenses and revisioning economics by bringing back the imagination, soul, and the feminine, including restoring Themis and Hestia to their rightful places. Interestingly, *The Oresteia* was one of the productions featured in the 2019 Epidaurus Festival, held at the ancient theater in Epidaurus, Greece. It was as if Greece was reminding itself of its own ancient wisdom.

Images emerged from image-makers of all kinds—historians, entrepreneurs, government officials, and artists, particularly street artists. They revealed aspects of the shadow and shifts in perspective, including a loosening of the God-image and cultural complexes. The Greek people also seemed to be reimagining their history and reviving the feminine. There was a renewed interest in tending the place of Athens, reflecting a desire to nurture the collective psyche and soul. The people also seemed to remember that the antidote to the Titanic elements running the economic system is the presence of the other gods and goddesses. Zeus and the Olympic gods and goddesses submerged the Titans beneath the sea; "Titanic hugeness can be encompassed and contained only by an equally large capacity of inspired image-making" (Hillman, 2007, p. 148). During this time, I came across a painting by Charles Billich called *The Gods Return to Athens*, with images of the Olympic gods overlooking a mix of modern and ancient Athens. It felt like a fitting image for the events happening in Greece.

The Red Thread to Restoring and Revisioning Economics

The Greek people and government directly addressed some shadow aspects hindering their economic health. SYRIZA, the political party that governed during most of the crisis, conducted a post-mortem on its own shortcomings in managing the crisis. It acknowledged that it ignored reality, lacked critical knowledge of the financial system and the Greek public sector, and failed to present a vision for the future (SYRIZA Concedes Mistakes, 2020). Toward the end of the crisis, the Greek people also voted for a more moderate leader, Kyriakos Mitsotakis. Some argue he has made Greece more business-friendly by cutting red tape and supporting entrepreneurial activity, possibly signs of a healthier senex and puer. He also modernized several aspects of the government, including revamping "the way citizens interact with the state, thanks to an impressive digitalization programme" (Only, 2023, p. 44). Others are more critical of his efforts to modernize public services and the justice system, which remains "Byzantine and creaking" (p. 44). His government is also not without scandals and cronyism. Greece is performing better by current economic metrics, such as increased GDP and foreign investment, alongside decreased debt, although the latter remains high. However, there are concerns about whether this growth is healthy and sustainable, as it relies heavily on the precarious and invasive tourist industry. Some Greek people are still struggling financially.

As noted throughout the book, economics suffers from a crisis in imagination, a lack of the feminine, and a neglect of the instinctual. These elements are found in the myth of Medusa, the monstrous woman with snakes for hair who turns men to stone. This was the final gift of the red thread in my exploration of the GFC. One day, while contemplating the relevance of Medusa's myth to economics, I took a break to go out and buy a new pair of running shoes. I noticed a flash of a tattoo peeking out from the sleeve of the salesperson who was assisting me. I asked him about it, and he lifted his sleeve; it depicted Perseus holding Medusa's severed head.

Before she became grotesque, Medusa was a beautiful maiden whom Poseidon violated in Athena's temple. The offended Athena punished Medusa for this act by transforming her into a terrifying creature. From an archetypal perspective, the myth is often interpreted as reflecting a double patriarchal wounding of the feminine. Medusa is assaulted by the masculine and punished for the masculine's sins by the goddess Athena, known for her strong ties to masculine power. Consequently, an aspect of the feminine becomes wild and controlling, and because she cannot be integrated or tamed, Medusa must be killed.

The myth also highlights the dynamics between civilization and the instinctual. Medusa is mortal, and Poseidon, who reflects instinctual nature, invades the temple of the civilized Athena and violently happens upon Medusa, much like the unconscious and the instinctual happen upon humans, sometimes violently and seemingly without control. Civilization, represented by Athena in the myth, condemns this and binds the instinctual and the feminine together, keeping them held hostage in a violent monstrosity. This reflects the cost of civilization: the repression of various seemingly unruly aspects, which only makes them more monstrous and controlling in the shadows. Medusa is the unfortunate victim. This dynamic is observed clearly in many Westernized, Christian god-images. Civilization becomes one-sided as the feminine, unconscious, and instinctual are rejected, along with the richness they contribute.

Perseus beheads Medusa by wearing Hades' cap of invisibility and Hermes' winged sandals and gazing at Medusa through the reflection in Athena's shield. Upon doing so, the winged bull Chrysaor and the winged horse Pegasus, who reflects creativity, emerge from her neck. Slaying the monster created from trauma and shunning the feminine and instinctual is essential for unleashing the imagination.

The image of Medusa's head became a protective talisman that Athena wore on her armor breastplate. This symbolizes the strength gained from integrating shadow aspects and overcoming trauma. They transform from something monstrous in the shadows into strength and protection. It is important to note that, like the hero Perseus, who uses Athena's shield for reflection, people often must face their traumas and shadows indirectly, avoiding a direct confrontation. Otherwise, they could be turned into stone. As Trousdell noted, they must be worked with symbolically, which the ancient Greek people seemed to understand.

Greek Lessons in Transformation

Cultural events during the Greek crisis brought the arts, the imagination, and play to work with archetypal dyads, open wounds, and the shadow. Two cultural centers opened during the crisis: The Stavros Niarchos Foundation Cultural Center and the Onassis Stegi. Jung also clearly understood the importance of culture, which is slowly being realized by government leaders: "Governments around the world are turning to the arts as a means to spur economic regeneration" (Bullt, 2023, p. 68).

The Museum of Cycladic Art (2019) In Athens exhibited Picasso's work, which reflects the dynamics between Apollo and Dionysus. Picasso's work specifically emphasized the need to hold the tension between the two as "the Apollonian emphasizes nature's benevolent force, light, the linear, and the sculptural; the Dionysian, on the other hand, stems from the raw animality, the unconscious, darkness, and freedom" (para. 2).

In 2012, a new arts and culture journal, *South as a State of Mind,* was created with a mission to overcome the stereotypes associated with the South such as "perfect climate, easy living, chaos, corruption, and the dramatic temperament" (South as a State of Mind, n.d., para. 1). The National Museum of Contemporary Art (2018–2019) hosted the exhibit, *The Ballad of Forgotten Places* in collaboration with the Italian council. It highlighted the inequities fragmenting Europe (Fonazaione Merz website, n.d.).

The U.S. and Greece both seemed to flirt with viewing the world through a terrapsychological lens. In 2017, Guillermo del Toro's film *The Shape of*

Water captivated the imagination of the U.S., winning many awards. The film reveals the U.S.'s Cartesian, Christian, and violent shadows through the antagonist, Colonel Strickland. The protagonist, Princess Elisa, revealed an enchanted way of engaging with Nature (Smith, 2019).

Parts of Athens were renovated, including Omonia (Harmony) Square, which was the heart of Athens in the mid-1800s but had deteriorated to one of the dingiest parts of Athens "a tree-less, water-less, fountain-less cesspool of graffiti, human trafficking, filth, crime, open drug dealing and prostitution" (Dabilis, 2012, para. 2). The government renovated it in 2020 and launched a cleanup campaign for other parts of Athens. The mayor of Athens, Kostas Bakoyannis, noted that "what is changing in the capital is [people's] understanding of the need for daily life to be civilized" (Municipal Crews Clean Up, 2020, para. 4). Caring for places also nurtures the communal soul.

The sacred place of Demeter and Persephone was also cultivated. Despite being one of the most important religious sites of ancient times, Eleusis, now modern-day Elefsina, became one of the most industrial, polluted parts of Greece: "a graveyard for abandoned factories and decommissioned ships" (Korachai, 2016). However, in 2021, it was named the European Capital of Culture. As a result, plans were created to renovate Eleusis, which seemed to stir the economic imagination and hopefully bring the powerful goddesses back into the cultural god-image:

> Elefsina addresses the issues that concern Europe, like development, social cohesion and, ultimately, prosperity. Humankind has experienced two major transitions so far: the agricultural and the industrial revolutions. Today we face the fresh challenge of finding a new model for sustainable development and we are presenting a town that, despite all its problems, is investing in culture.
>
> (Korachai, 2016, para. 14)

As discussed throughout the book, street art played a prominent role during the crisis by reflecting the hardships and envisioning new ways of being. For instance, various images of a king's head with the words "Kings Are Dead" and "Kings Are Deader Than Dead" appeared on the city walls of Athens. In fairy tales, the king often symbolizes the ego, and a dying king signifies the death of an old way of being. Thus, the street art may have indicated a loosening of the old ways. Additionally, a desire to rid society of an oppressive patriarchal presence is depicted in a work by barba.dee, featuring a burning house with the phrase "Burn Down the Patriarchy" written underneath.

The artist, Dimitris Ntokos, created various images of scarab beetles. Beetles roll dung balls through subterranean tunnels for food or to lay their eggs. Their digestion of excrement and its use as a source of nourishment or reproduction serves as an interesting metaphor for the value of processing the shadow and the new life it can foster. A sense of renewal is depicted in a large mural in the soulful neighborhood of Exarchia. It shows people and seeds beneath the earth, which grow into beautiful sun-like plants that break through the city's concrete.

Greece also demonstrated bringing together the senex and puer to reimagine history. In the fall of 2019, at the National History Museum, historians used thousands of Legos to create scenes depicting the Greek War of Independence—perhaps an attempt to process the unhealed trauma through play and imagination. There was also a revival of the old gods for modern times in museum gift shops. For many years, the selection of items was limited, outdated, and controlled by the government, which is significant as "the gift shops operating at Greece's museums and archaeological sites sum up the Culture Ministry's idea of promoting the country's cultural heritage" (Sykka, 2019, para. 1). However, during the crisis, despite governmental red tape, several contemporary products were created for the gift shops based on ancient artifacts. A further loosening of the senex in the shadows was seen in the 2019 National Theater production of *A Christmas Carol*, which explored the transformation of a greedy, miserly senex into someone more generous and concerned with relationships and people's well-being.

The connection between the Acropolis and the psyche of the Greek people was explored in 2019 at the Kalfayan Gallery with a desire to both honor its original symbolic meaning and to consider how it may need to evolve, bringing together the senex and the puer. The artists of *The Past of the Future* exhibit consider the symbolism of the Acropolis contemplating the questions "in what ways is such a strong symbol imprinted in the Greek Psyche but also in the collective unconscious in time of crisis? How could it be re-conceptualized in contemporary history?" (Kalfayan Galleries, n.d., para. 2). The artists call out the commercialism of the Acropolis and recognize it for being a "universal symbol of the classical spirit and democracy" (para. 1).

The Greek people also sought to bring in other gods and goddesses, such as Themis, Hestia, and Aphrodite, to confront the enormity of the Titans. Elements of Hestia and Themis can be found at a Center dedicated to Hestia in Athens's beautiful Nea Smyrni neighborhood. The center was established to unite the community following the Greece-Turkey population exchange in the 1920s. The center, directed by Themis for over 40 years, preserves the memories of the conflicts between Turkey and Greece and serves as a community hub, offering space for children to play sports and perform theater. It holds space for the past and the future.

There appeared to be efforts to cultivate Athena in Greek culture. The official 2019 good-luck charm of the Acropolis Museum was inspired by an image from Athena's first temple. Depth psychologists have frequently suggested that Athena embodies a more masculine-oriented woman; she was born from Zeus's head and was known to assist Greek heroes. However, Downing (2007) also posited that Athena is connected to the soul and the Underworld, helping us to overcome the repression of the feminine as a soul-task (p. 114).

Athena also rescued Dionysus's heart when he was destroyed by the Titans. Her presence is needed in economics.

The Greek people supported other aspects of the feminine. There were several exhibits in museums and galleries either created by women artists or featuring women in art. An exhibit at the National Archaeological Museum explored the importance of beauty, the body, and Aphrodite in ancient times. An exhibit at the Benaki museum by the artist Jannis Varelas built on Jung's idea of the anima, the female archetype found in men, in his exhibit *Anima 1* which focused on human creativity and the need for connection to the body and sexuality (Charitou, n.d.).

In his award-winning short film, *City of Athens: A Portrait of a* Changing Metropolis, Maragos (2018) invites in the gods and goddesses. In the opening image, Athens is in the distance against a backdrop of mountains, sea, and the setting sun. The music, *The Darkest Night*, begins. When the sun sets, the city's lights turn on. Signs of life appear in car headlights, illuminated hotel rooms, and computer screens flickering in office buildings. Planes fly alongside rolling clouds and Zeus's lightning bolts. Distant images of individual people in their cars and homes create a sense of community and oneness. Hestia and Themis feel present. The music picks up in tempo. Images of the university and library emerge. Lights illuminate the Acropolis and the Parthenon. A proud statue of Athena stands in her glory beneath the transiting moon, symbolizing Artemis, followed by statues of other ancient figures. Maragos captures footage of the two new cultural centers. The film concludes with the sun rising over the city. Athens feels whole and complete and filled with the gods and goddesses.

These are only a few examples of the many events, but they provide some idea of the power of the arts and the imagination. As Hillman (1976) said, "Greece is where our culture began" (p. 27). Greece is known as the birthplace of human civilization and seems to guide the current need for re-civilization through real heroism, the imagination, and tending soul. Even though I have studied Greece extensively, writing the book reminded me of Greece's gifts for, and the power of, culture and imagination, which seem part of its genius loci. As always, I hope I have done Greece and the Greek people justice.

A View Forward

In concluding the book, I recognize that much more could be said about Jung, mythology, and economics. I have only scratched the surface. As someone once told me, 40,000 words merely clears the throat. However, although brief, the red thread led us into rich territory while exploring the foundational issues of economics and envisioning new possibilities through a Jungian and mythological lens.

This book has been focused on looking back, and in wrapping up the book, it makes sense to look forward. When I think of where to go from here in early 2025, I feel overwhelmed. Much work is still to be done to advance the field of economics and enhance global economic health. The efforts of the economic movements like feminist economics, ecological economics, and Rethinking Economics must continue. Hopefully, I have demonstrated how depth psychology can be an ally in their missions by uncovering the psychological roots at the core of economic dysfunctions. As discussed extensively, a Jungian lens shows the need to value the anima mundi, address cultural wounds, confront the collective shadow, and enlarge the cultural God-image for economic health.

Changes need to be made on policy and legislative levels to fix the dysfunctions in the economic system, such as addressing neocolonialism, income inequalities, and environmental destruction. What is measured and valued when assessing economic health needs to be reconsidered, and neglected aspects of community well-being must be rescued from the shadows. In some ways, this depends on the people in charge: the politicians, policymakers, and influential businesspeople—aspects of civilization that are often not very civilized. However, as Greece clearly demonstrated, the power of culture cannot be underestimated. Working together to heal collective wounds, to care for places and the environment, and to honor the archetypal elements such as Themis, Hestia, Athena, and Dionysus can be helpful to counter the power of the Titanic and to care for the soul.

References

"Built to Order." (2023, April 8). *The Economist.*

Charitou, K. (n.d.). Jannis Varelas. *Artforum.* Retrieved from https://www.artforum.com/events/jannis-varelas-246136/

Dabilis, A. (2012, April 13). Yet another idea to restore the deteriorating Omonia Square. *Greek Reporter.* Retrieved from https://greece.greekreporter.com/2012/04/13/yet-another-idea-to-restore-the-deteriorating-omonia-square/

Downing, C. (2007). *The goddess: Mythological images of the feminine.* Authors Choice Press.

Fonazaione Merz website. (n.d.). https://fondazionemerz.org/en/exhibitions/bottobruno-the-ballad-of-forgotten-places-a-project-winner-of-italian-council/

Hillman, J. (1976). *Re-visioning psychology.* Harper & Row.

Hillman, J. (with Slater, G.). (2005). *Senex & puer.* G. Slater (Ed.). Spring Publications.

Hillman, J. (2007). *Mythic figures.* Spring Publications, Inc.

Johnson, R. A. (1986). *Inner work: Using dreams and active imagination for personal growth.* HarperCollins.

Jung, C. G. (1968). Religious ideas in alchemy (R. F. C. Hull, Trans.). In H. Read et al. (Eds.), *The collected works of C. G. Jung: Vol. 12. Psychology and alchemy* (2nd ed., pp. 225–472). Princeton University Press (Original work published 1937).

Kalfayan Galleries. (n.d.). https://www.kalfayangalleries.com/index23en.htm

Korachai, M. (2016, December 22). Eleusis: Mysterious ancient town named European culture capital. *Greece Is.* Retrieved from https://www.greece-is.com/elefsina-mysterious-ancient-town-named-european-culture-capital/

Maragos, A. (2018). *City of Athens: A portrait of a changing metropolis* [Video file]. Retrieved from https://alexandrosmaragos.com/city-of-athens

Miller, J. (2004). *The transcendent function*. SUNY Press.

Municipal Crews Clean up Exarchia, Kolonaki Squares. (2020, February 4). *Ekathimerini*. Retrieved from https://www.ekathimerini.com/249150/article/ekathimerini/news/municipal-crews-clean-up-exarchia-kolonaki-squares

Museum of Cycladic Art. (2019 June 20–2019 October 20). *Picasso and antiquity: Line and clay*. Athens.

National Museum of Contemporary Art. (2018 December 4–2019 January 20). *The ballad of forgotten places*. Athens.

"Only the First Round Beckons". (2023, April 22). *The Economist*.

Smith, J. D. (2019, March). The shape of water: An ecopsychological fairy tale. *Ecopsychology*, *11*(1), 43–48. https://www.liebertpub.com/doi/full/10.1089/eco.2018.0064

South as a State of Mind. (n.d.). https://southasastateofmind.com/about/

Sykka, I. (2019, May 16). Museum shops get facelift despite red tape. *Ekathimerini*. Retrieved from https://www.ekathimerini.com/240512/article/ekathimerini/life/museum-shops-get-facelift-despite-red-tape

Syriza Concedes Mistakes in Critical Review. (2020, February 12). *Ekathimerini*. Retrieved from https://www.ekathimerini.com/249434/article/ekathimerini/news/syriza-concedes-mistakes-in-critical-review

Trousdell, R. (2011). Surviving trauma, becoming human: Victim and hero roles in the Oresteia of Aeschylus. In V. Beane Rutter & T. Singer (Eds.), *Ancient Greece, modern psyche: Archetypes in the making* (pp. 131–158). Spring Journal Books.

Index

Acropolis 41, 42, 89, 90
alchemy 73, 82–83
Ananke 18, 25, 26
anima mundi 5–6, 8, 35, 38, 82, 91
Aphrodite 38, 41, 44, 78, 89, 90
Apollo 17–19, 27, 39, 61, 63–65, 82, 84, 87
archetypes 4–7, 15, 21, 38, 39, 48, 52, 58, 60, 70, 84, 90
art 1, 15, 17, 36, 40–43, 49, 59–61, 64, 73, 83, 85, 87–90
Athena 44, 52, 62–64, 84–87, 89–91
Athens 1, 16, 17, 37, 41–44, 48, 50, 61, 78, 85, 88–90

behavioral economics 3, 20–21
benevolent sexism 74–75
Big Short 25, 53

Cartesian culture 2, 6–7, 35, 65, 81, 88
Christianity 6, 16, 64, 66, 69, 71–79
co-evolution/co-creation 37, 70
collective unconscious 4, 7, 56, 88
complexes 3–4, 7–8, 21, 43, 53, 56
corruption 24, 28–30, 33, 50, 61
credit 13, 20, 25, 26, 51
cultural complexes 5, 8–9, 49–50, 56–66, 69, 81, 84, 85
cultural unconscious 35, 70, 79

debt 13, 18, 20, 24–25, 29, 30, 50, 63, 86
defenses 47–48, 52–54, 85
Demeter 37, 44, 78, 88
Dionysus 38, 41, 52, 61–63, 65–66, 71, 73, 82, 87, 91
dreams 7, 15, 48, 70

ecological economics 20, 91
efficiency 13, 27
ego 13, 19, 43, 47–48, 51, 53–54, 62, 76, 82, 83, 88
Eleusis 37, 88
emotion 3, 7, 8, 10, 15, 17, 18, 20–21, 27, 37, 38, 47, 52, 56, 57, 60–63, 71, 84
entrepreneurship 30, 62, 78, 85, 86

fairness 27, 32
feminine 36, 62, 65, 71–75, 78, 79, 81, 82, 84–87, 89–90
feminist economics 20, 91
film 25, 64, 87, 90
Furies 84–85

genius loci 36–39, 44, 51, 81, 90
Germany 29, 42, 59–66, 69, 71, 73, 84
God-image 1, 9, 69–79, 81–82, 85, 91
government ineffectiveness 24–33, 38, 42, 50, 61–62, 78–79, 85–86

Hades 4, 87; *see also* Underworld
Hephaestus 49
Hermes 18, 25, 30, 39, 40, 61, 63, 87
hero 2, 16, 21, 40, 47, 48, 50–54, 60–63, 76, 77, 84–85. 90
Hestia 18, 20, 25, 32, 38–40, 42, 44, 81, 85, 89–91
Highway to Hellas 64–65
housing 1, 24–26, 38–39, 44

images 14–15, 60, 77
imagination 3, 4, 7, 13–15, 25, 32, 46–48, 62, 72, 79, 81, 82, 85–90
individualism 20
individuation 4–5, 58, 71, 82, 83
instinctual 4, 35, 53, 62, 65, 66, 71, 73, 78, 79, 82, 86–87
intuition 4, 21

justice 26–27, 39, 72, 84, 86, 90

King Midas 12–13

Lenape 39–40, 44

Manhattan 39–41
masculine 3, 19, 20, 36, 71, 74, 78, 82, 86, 89
Medusa 86–87
Minotaur 2, 26
Moneta 15
mythology 2, 3, 7, 40

Nature 5–6, 8, 15–17, 19, 20, 35–44
neocolonialism 65, 91
North 65–66, 82

Oikonomia 18, 35
Oresteia 84–85
Orthodox Church 31–32, 52, 69, 75–79
Ottoman rule 32, 42

Pegasus 87
Persephone 37, 78, 88
Poseidon 86
projection 7–8, 60, 64, 66
puer 40, 43, 59, 64, 65, 74, 79, 82–84, 86, 89

religion 69–71
Rethinking Economics 20–21, 91

Saturn/Senex 17, 18, 26, 30, 36, 38–40, 62–65, 72–74, 78–79, 82–84, 86, 89
shadow 3–5, 7–8, 18, 19, 38, 47, 50–53, 58–66
soul 2, 5–7, 13–19, 36–38, 43–44, 48, 51, 65, 69, 72–73, 77–78, 82, 84, 85, 88–91
South 26, 65, 82, 87
spirit 5, 14–16, 18, 36, 65, 71–72, 77, 82
spiritus loci *see* genius loci
street art 1, 17, 41, 43, 49, 60, 61, 64, 85, 88–89
suffering 1, 4, 5, 12, 27, 31, 40, 42–44, 47–48, 50–52, 62, 73, 77–78, 81, 84–85
symbolic approach 7, 14, 17, 37, 43, 47, 58, 71, 73, 81, 85, 87
synchronicity 1, 8, 70
systemic view 13, 36, 40, 59

tax evasion 28–31, 33, 61, 76
terrapsychology 37–44, 87
Themis 26–27, 39–41, 44, 74, 81, 85, 89–91
titanism 17, 25, 35, 38, 40, 44, 52, 53, 58, 59, 61–62, 65, 66, 75, 77, 82, 85, 89–91
transcendent function 82–83, 85
transformation 1, 8, 20, 32, 47, 52, 59–60, 62–63, 66, 70–72, 77–79, 81–91
trauma 3, 8, 28, 37, 42–44, 46–54, 56, 58, 72–73, 77–79, 81, 84–85, 87, 89
Troika 28–31, 50, 51

unconscious 3–4, 7–8, 15, 21, 37, 46, 47, 54, 56–57, 62, 65, 66, 70, 75–77, 79, 81–84, 86–87, 89
Underworld 4, 37, 40, 891; *see also* Hades
unus mundus 6, 8

Varoufakis, Y. 26, 51, 61

Wall Street 26, 39–40, 66, 73, 75, 81
World War II 42, 43, 51

Zeus 17, 38, 50, 52, 62, 63, 66, 85, 89, 90

www.ingramcontent.com/pod-product-compliance
Lightning Source LLC
LaVergne TN
LVHW011513200926
848484LV00001B/30
9781032805993